BLESSED IS THE MAN

A LEGACY OF FAITH AND FAMILY VALUES

DONALD DARNELL HARPER

WITH ABIGALE BELCHER OGDEN

Blessed Is the Man: A Legacy of Faith and Family Values

All Scripture references are taken from the English Standard Version unless otherwise noted.

ISBN: 978-1-940645-41-4

 COURIER PUBLISHING

Greenville, South Carolina

Praise for 'Blessed Is the Man'

In late summer of 2015, I received a telephone call from a man that I did not know. He told me that he had grown up in Marion, Alabama, where I had, also. He said, "I want to thank you for something your father did for my mother and father."

This is a story about faith and trust. It is a story about a family and a story about two men — one black, one white. Their lives paralleled each other, for they both strove to better themselves and their families.

Thank you, Don Harper, for not only honoring your parents, but for honoring my father and the Marion Bank and Trust Company.

Geneva Blackburn
Marion, Alabama

On an internal quest to explain his life to the world, Donald Darnell Harper focuses his intellectual insight on the lives of his parents, those two remarkable individuals whose success many families strive to duplicate. What is the difference between those individuals who do something special — touching or influencing so many others — versus those who just seem to accept life as it is? Mr. Harper explains how the habits of highly successful people pale in importance to where, when, and how they were raised.

This story is a pleasure to read and will leave you pondering how this was possible during that particular time in the deep South. It is a must-read for all cultures, from educators to parents.

Lee A. Benson
Dayton, Ohio

FOREWORD

There are moments every day that offer us the opportunity for something great to happen. Indeed, the plan has already been made for us to have these experiences. We may not see the plan in its entirety, or even in its parts while in the moment — but God has laid the plan for our interaction, and what those interactions will mean in the history of our life and our legacy to this world. All we need to do is be open to the glory that is life, and, in the interest of God's will, remain vulnerable to the people who are placed along our path. Through this vulnerability, we expose our soul to connect with another person through God's greater plan.

In 2012, I had the pleasure to meet a gentleman in just such a way. I was running late to our meeting, and when I entered the room I felt an immediate sensation of connectedness. I could not place my finger, or feelings, on that sensation, but I knew that in my efforts to remain open to interaction, I was being given a gift in this moment. He carried a strong and deep presence, almost intimidating, but warm at the same time. Immediately, I was drawn to him and to the meaning for our meeting this day.

During our discussion of business, our conversation drifted to personal matters and background history. The normal and casual questions of "What brought you to this area?" or "What do you do for a living?" were briefly discussed. Through this conversation and discussion of his work background and mentoring of youth, I was drawn in further. I mentioned that this mentoring was something that we have seemingly lost so much of in our current society and is a great blessing for those to whom he gives of himself. He gave credit to his parents, who, through their spiritual beliefs and values, believed in doing right by others. Then he opened up about his family history and began talking further in depth about his father. He spoke of growing up as an African-American in rural Alabama on a farm that his father owned and how the family unit survived in those deeply segregated times. Unfortunately for my great interest, our visit was cut short by necessity for other scheduled meetings.

Several years later, we reconnected at another meeting. Again, I was running late and felt a little uneasy as I entered the room in hopes that he would not be impatient with my tardiness. As I entered the room, I remembered immediately his face and his family story from two years prior. I shook his hand and sat down in a chair across from him, and before even thinking of the business reasons for today's meeting, I asked him to tell me more about his father. He replied, "What do you mean, my father?" I said, "If you don't mind, I'd like to hear more about the farm and how your family survived and thrived." He was taken aback and said, somewhat surprised at himself, "I told you about my father?" I told him that his story had intrigued me and had been on my mind intermittently since our first visit. We spoke for an unknown duration of time, but I was so beguiled by the depth of the family history and the presence of faith his family had that I said it would be a shame for that history to be lost from the next generation. It needed to be shared.

God plants the seeds and then places people in our lives to help water them.

Since then, we have met several times for business, and, each time, there has been a reason for our visit that went beyond business. Each time, the personal or spiritual reason for our visit could only be explained through the manifestation of faith in the greater plan of God through placing people in our lives at the right time for the right reason. The personal meaning of those interactions have left an indelible mark on my life and in my spiritual journey as a man.

As the story of the depth of this family's faith in God and their faith in each other unfolds through the words on these pages, I pray you will allow yourself the vulnerability to let the history touch your heart in a way that is meaningful and lasting. The fortitude to live through history in this manner, and the courage to tell the story unabashedly and with great reverence to God the Creator, gives magic to our world and faith to our soul.

Daniel Boxwell, DO
Seneca, South Carolina

Remembering Mom Harper

In August of 1966, I was already engaged to Don ("Darnell," the baby, to his family), when I met Mom Harper at the old homestead. I was grateful for her warm welcome, knowing the attachment that must have existed between a mother and her youngest son. I was quite surprised two days later when we were alone at the dining room table and she said, "I can learn to share him if you can!" I said, "Yes ma'am, I can!" From that day forward, I made it my goal to love her and give her the time and space she needed with her "baby."

The Lord blessed us in 1974 when, because of Don's job, we moved to Alabama, 150 miles from Mom. We got to see her at least once a month and even more during gardening season. I enjoyed our trips together into town, and I loved worshipping with her. Even today, when we enter that church in Marion, I can picture her wearing her pretty hats and sitting on her favorite bench.

Mom had lots of stories to share, and one of her tales definitely changed how I ride in a car. It was about two people riding down a country road with their windows down. Mom said a rattlesnake jumped into the car and landed between the two people! No more windows down in the car for me, even if the air conditioner is broken!

Mom was a great cook. I remember times spent with her in the kitchen. She taught me how to make pound cake and ice cream. She gave me the recipe for her famous Alabama Fruit Cake. (The paper it is written on is splattered with some of the ingredients she used.) I have that recipe framed and hanging in my kitchen. I also have in my kitchen her butter churn, which I cherish.

I truly believe I became her second favorite daughter-in-law, and I was happy with that!

Dad Harper passed away before I met Don, but I believe I have met him through my husband. When I look at Dad Harper's picture, I see Don. And from what people have told me about Dad Harper, Don is a great representative of him. They say Dad Harper was a godly man who loved his wife, his kids and his fellow man.

Both Mom and Dad Harper left a great legacy of faith and family. They were great lights for Christ in the Marion community. Thank you, honey, for telling their story. And thank you, "Doctor B," for encouraging Don to do so.

Gerri Harper

Introduction

The idea of a legacy is a powerful thing. A legacy is the part of you that remains on earth long after your soul has passed into eternity. It goes far beyond the wealth you have amassed or the accomplishments you have attained. It is how you live on in memory; it is the sum of every difference you have made in the lives of others during your lifetime. Silver and gold, houses and whatnot, don't really matter, but a legacy will endure.

To a certain extent, you will never know exactly what people will remember about you after you are gone; however, each of us has the ability to live his or her life in a manner such that any aspect of it might be remembered favorably. For a Christian, the best possible legacy he or she can leave is that of a God-honoring, loving, selfless life.

It starts out with a commitment to Christ and to living according to His standards on a daily basis. It also means making sure you're not tempted to go off the path one way or another, because no matter how long you spend building a reputation, it could be gone like that. I challenge people to build up their reputations because they owe it, if not to themselves, then at least to their children.

The words of Proverbs 3:1-6 aptly express the importance of a Christian legacy and echo the lessons taught to me by my own parents: "My son, do not forget my teaching, but let your heart keep my commandments [...]. Let not steadfast love and faithfulness forsake you; bind them around your neck; write them on the tablet of your heart so you will find favor and good success in the sight of God and man. Trust in the Lord with all your heart, and do not lean on your own understanding. In all your ways acknowledge him, and he will make straight your paths."

Mom and Dad have been gone for many years now, and we kids have long since grown up and become parents and grandparents ourselves, but the lessons learned while we were living and working together on the farm have stayed with me and continue to impact the way I live my life. I have had the opportunity to talk about my parents' legacy in speeches and interviews, but never before in a format that has such potential to reach so many people.

There is undeniably a personal desire to preserve the memory of Lloyd and Walter Mae Harper for all of their descendants. I want my children and grandchildren and nieces and nephews to know where they come from and what a rich heritage of faith is in their past. If strangers are telling stories about Mom and Dad, then their grandchildren certainly ought to be telling stories about Mom and Dad.

I also believe that the example of a man and woman who dedicated their lives to God's glory can have an impact far beyond their own family and even their hometown community. Both of my parents on countless occasions illustrated biblical truths by simply staying true to their convictions. The active and passive lessons they taught me are ones I think have the potential to benefit believers everywhere.

This book is not the work of a great theologian or a seasoned pastor. The truths presented here are simply what the Holy Spirit has shown me through Scripture reading, prayer, and personal reflection, with guidance from other works written by godly men who have poured their lives into biblical studies. I therefore encourage you to respond to the questions at the end of each chapter freely and confidently.

It is my desire that this book be a source of wisdom and encouragement for all, that each person who reads it would glean truth to apply to his or her own life. You see, these are more than just stories of an African-American family in Alabama; these are testimonies to the goodness and provision of the Almighty God. The love and grace He showed us is the same that He shows all His children. Therefore, the godly path that my parents trod and that I now endeavor to follow them on is one that I would invite you to also follow.

Donald Darnell Harper
November 2016

TABLE OF CONTENTS

Walter Mae and Lloyd Harper, Sr.

CHAPTER ONE

BLESSINGS (ALMOST) BEYOND BELIEF

I firmly believe that every skill, talent, and resource you have or will acquire comes as a gift from God. He gives these gifts freely out of His abundant love for us; we could never earn nor truly deserve any of God's blessings, which makes the measure of them all the more overwhelming.

Now, when I say "God," I do not mean a grandfatherly figure who sits on a cloud and dispenses nice things whenever we ask; nor do I mean a heartless tyrant who waits for us to make the slightest mistake so that he can strike us down. Neither of those images is accurate in describing the God of the Bible. Who, then, is God?

The first image the Bible gives us of God is that of Creator. Genesis 1:1 says, "In the beginning, God created the heavens and the earth"; the rest of the chapter describes how he brought all things into existence, from the tiniest creatures that creep upon the earth to the massive stars that light the night sky, and all of that within the span of six days. It is hard to imagine, but John 1:3 tells us that there was literally *nothing* before God: "All things were made through him, and without him was not any thing made that was made."

In other words, God has always existed; whereas all other things have a beginning and end, God is infinite, dwelling simultaneously in the past, present, and future. Not only that, but He dwells in all places at all times. Psalm 139:7-10 describes God's omnipresence in very personal terms: "Where shall I go from your Spirit? Or where shall I flee from your presence? If I ascend to heaven, you are there! If I make my bed in Sheol, you are there! If I take the wings of the morning and dwell in the uttermost parts of the sea, even there your hand shall lead me, and your right hand shall hold me."

The Lord Himself declared His magnitude to the prophet Jeremiah when He said, "'Am I only a God nearby, […] and not a God far away? Who can hide in secret places so that I cannot see them? […] Do not I fill heaven and earth?'" (Jeremiah 23:23-24, NIV).

That God's presence spans and infinitely exceeds the universe should fill us with awe. He is a being (the only being) without limitation; however, to know that He exists in the farthest reaches of space is also to know that He is very near. We never need worry that God has abandoned us or forgotten us or lost track of us. He is in control and ever mindful of the big picture, but He is also Lord over the small moments. As Jesus said to His disciples, "Are not two sparrows sold for a penny? Yet not one of them will fall to the ground outside your Father's care. And even the very hairs of your head are all numbered. So don't be afraid; you are worth more than many sparrows" (Matthew 10:29-31, NIV).

The Lord also declares Himself to be holy, and His followers testify to His righteousness (the outward expression of His holiness) throughout Scripture. The psalmist says that God's righteousness "reaches to the heavens" (71:19), that it is "everlasting" (119:142, NIV), that it is the "foundation of [His] throne" (97:2). The prophet Isaiah said that God would be shown to be holy through His righteous acts. In the New Testament, the apostle Paul wrote that our ability to have redemption through Jesus Christ demonstrates God's righteousness because He can be both "just and the justifier of the one who has faith in Jesus" (Romans 3:23-26); and in Revelation 15:4, John records his vision of the servants of God still testifying to the Lord's righteousness in earth's last days: "Who will not fear, O Lord, and glorify your name? For you alone are holy. All nations will come and worship you, for your righteous acts have been revealed."

Clearly, righteousness is an important attribute of God's nature, but what does it mean to say that God is righteous or holy? We can imagine examples of virtue; and indeed we are to think about virtuous things because they reflect the character of our Lord. But one cannot simply say that God is virtuous. He is the definition of virtue. As A.W. Tozer writes in his book *The Knowledge of the Holy*, "We cannot grasp the true meaning of the divine holiness by thinking of someone or something very pure and then raising the concept to the highest degree we are capable of. God's holiness is not simply the best we know infinitely bettered. [...] It stands apart, unique, unapproachable, incomprehensible and unattainable. [...] To be holy He does not conform to a standard. He *is* that standard."[1]

Because God is the absolute standard of what is good, it follows that what is not of God is not good. That is what is meant by the term "sin." That which is not good prevents us from sharing perfect communion with God as He desires. Just as an extramarital affair would create a barrier between husband and wife, so our sin stands between us and God. As it is written in Isaiah

59:1-2, "Behold, the Lord's hand is not shortened, that it cannot save, or his ear dull, that it cannot hear; but your iniquities have made a separation between you and your God, and your sins have hidden his face from you so that he does not hear."

You may think, "There shouldn't be anything in the way between God and me. I have never done anything *really* bad." If that is your response, let me ask you a couple of questions. Have you ever been angry at someone? Jesus himself said, "But I say to you that everyone who is angry with his brother will be liable to judgment ..." (Matthew 5:22).

Jesus also said that everyone who lusts after another has already committed adultery with that person in his heart, and who among us has not had less-than-holy thoughts about a woman or man at some point? At the very least, we are all unquestionably guilty of idolatry, because we have all chosen at some point to raise someone or something other than God to the position of primary importance in our lives.

Since we all struggle with the same selfish tendencies, we tend to excuse many of them in each other. As Tozer puts it, "Until we have seen ourselves as God see us, we are not likely to be much disturbed over conditions around us as long as they do not get so far out of hand as to threaten our comfortable way of life. We have learned to live with unholiness and have come to look upon it as the natural and expected thing."[2]

No matter what culture or instinct tells us, the Bible says that we are all responsible for our wrongdoing, and the penalty for sin is death. Romans 5:12 tells us, "Sin came into the world through one man, and death through sin, and so death spread to all men because all sinned." If death seems a harsh consequence for any transgression, remember that God's standard is absolute: James 2:10 tells us, "For whoever keeps the whole law but fails in one point has become guilty of all of it."

Knowing that all are guilty and subject to the judgment of a perfectly just God, what can we do to fix it? In short, nothing. There is nothing we can do to make ourselves right with God, because we are incapable of perfectly following His commandments. But just when our situation seems impossible, we realize God has already made it possible to restore our relationship with Him: "For God so loved the world, that he gave his only Son, that whoever believes in him should not perish but have eternal life" (John 3:16).

This well-known verse, which records the words of

Jesus Himself, explains in simple terms the beautiful truth of the gospel. That the same God who created and reigns over the universe loves us and desires to have a relationship with us is amazing beyond words in and of itself. But God desired reconciliation with us so much that He sent His son, Jesus, to earth to be born of a virgin, to live a sinless life, to be crucified as payment for our sins, and to be raised from the dead so that we might have eternal life with Him in God's kingdom.

It is on Jesus that the foundation of our faith is built. Jesus is fully God, inexplicably united with God the Father in the Holy Trinity. Jesus is also fully man and able to understand the struggles of we, His creation, from firsthand experience. Hebrews 4:15 tells us, "For we do not have a high priest who is unable to sympathize with our weaknesses, but one who in every respect has been tempted as we are, yet without sin."

Jesus could not be punished for his own guilt, because there was nothing for which he was guilty; so His death on the cross satisfied the sentence of death for the sins of every man, woman, and child who lived then or has ever lived since. We no longer have to fear judgment from God, because he has already judged His own son in our place: "But he was pierced for our transgressions; he was crushed for our iniquities; upon him was the chastisement that brought us peace, and with his wounds we are healed" (Isaiah 53:5).

And so, this story of the blessings God has given to my family begins with the best and biggest blessing of all: the gift of salvation through Jesus Christ. As those who have believed in His saving grace, we are called to be God's ambassadors to the world, testifying to His goodness and grace and living every moment in an attitude that mirrors His. One man demonstrated God's love in a profound way that transformed the lives of my parents and of all their descendants.

~

Imagine that you are an African-American living in the segregated South in 1942, in the midst of the Jim Crow era, at the height of the Great Depression. You have no steady income, no savings, and no collateral — only a vision to purchase your own farm so your children do not have to grow up as sharecroppers. It was in the midst of those very circumstances that my dad went to the Marion Bank and Trust Company to ask for a loan to purchase eighty acres of prime farm land near Scott

Station in Perry County, Alabama.

The land was situated between two properties belonging to Caucasian men who, at that time, would have been assumed to be more trustworthy and therefore more likely to repay a debt. One was a dairy farmer who wanted the land to grow his business; the other was a cattle rancher who wanted to expand the grazing area of his herds. Both men had the advantage of being financially established. My parents had no resources at the time and no guaranteed prospects for the future. By every banking criterion, they were a risky investment at best. With all these factors at stake, it would seem impossible for my parents to realize their dream of owning land, but nothing is impossible with God.

At the bank, my dad waited patiently while the other (Caucasian) customers were served first. He didn't have

The Marion Bank and Trust Company as it appeared in 1942.

an appointment; it wasn't seen as socially acceptable in that culture for an African-American customer to request to be served before a Caucasian customer. Finally, when there was no one else to take priority, Dad was admitted in to speak with Jeff Blackburn, a teller at the bank.

Mr. Blackburn was not a friend or business associate; as far as I know, he was a complete stranger to my parents before that day. I do not know what was said in their conversation or what kind of business plan my dad laid out to demonstrate his reliability, but I do know that he left the bank with the loan he needed to purchase our farm approved.

Jeff Blackburn somehow convinced his superiors and the members of the bank's board of trust that they should finance this African-American farmer. Jeff

Jeff Blackburn, the man who helped my dad secure a loan to buy his farm, later became president of Marion Bank and Trust Company.

Blackburn acted on faith and served as the vehicle for God to provide for our family. Although doing the right thing was not "politically correct," Mr. Blackburn did what was biblically correct. Not only was Mr. Blackburn compassionate and caring, he was also innovative; he came up with a system for my father to repay the loan even without regular monthly income. Mr. Blackburn even arranged for the bank to advance Dad money each year to buy fertilizer and seed for the cotton and corn crops.

My parents never forgot the kindness shown to them. They remained grateful to God and His servant for as long as they lived, and they delighted to tell the story of the Lord's provision. Hearing that story all the time we were growing up prompted my siblings and me, many years later, to try to contact Mr. Blackburn's family. We were able to meet with Mr. Blackburn's daughter, Geneva Blackburn, and thank her on his behalf for his impact on our family.

God's Provision, Our Responsibility

This story, while demonstrating the extravagance of God's gifts, also highlights the faithfulness of two of God's men and provides a model for believers to follow. Both my dad and Mr. Blackburn presented good examples of what a Christian should do in response to the Lord's provision. Although God's love and our standing with Him are not dependent on our actions, a Christian should respond to God's gifting with gratitude and use those gifts for God's glory. The Bible makes it clear in 1 Peter 4:10 how we, as followers of Christ, are to use God's blessings: "As each has received a gift, use it to serve one another, as good stewards of God's varied grace … ."

This means that when God grants a gift to one person, it is meant to bless both that person and others through that person. Has He blessed you with extra time in your schedule? Consider spending some of that time volunteering with local ministries or visiting shut-ins. Has God blessed you with a skill or talent, such as accounting or working with children? Consider sharing those abilities with your church. Does your income exceed your daily needs? Consider using some of those extra funds to support mission work in foreign countries.

The Christians of the early church responded to God's generosity in very practical ways. The Book of Acts tells us that whenever there was a need, they gave generously to meet that need, even selling expensive possessions or property in order to provide for others. They believed that they were only stewards of God's good gifts, that the resources with which God had blessed them ultimately belonged to God and were thus to be used for His glory.

To be a steward is to be a caretaker, a trusted servant. A good steward recognizes the value of what has been entrusted to him and treats it with care out of love for his master. God provided a good job for Jeff Blackburn at the Marion Bank and Trust and opened doors for him to advance in the institution. Mr. Blackburn did not take lightly the opportunity given to him; instead, he honored the Lord in his life and used his position to bless others. I am sure that my dad was not the only bank client to have benefitted from Mr. Blackburn's kindness.

My dad showed himself to be a good steward of God's blessings, as well. Dad believed that one's word is one's bond; he expected others to deal with him honestly, and he stood behind any promise he made. Dad never missed a loan payment, and the balance was paid off well before the contract deadline. My dad demonstrated his gratitude to Mr. Blackburn and the other bank leaders by honoring his agreement.

Jeff Blackburn did not let the fear of what his

coworkers or community might think stop him from showing grace to an African-American couple. He acted on faith, obeying God's command to help those in need. God blessed Mr. Blackburn for his obedience by furthering his career and eventually opening the door for him to become president of the Marion Bank and Trust Company.

As Mr. Blackburn's experience proved, serving God does not return void. Romans 8:28 says, "And we know that for those who love God all things work together for good, for those who are called according to his purpose." Although "good" may not always mean a job promotion or a new home, we have the promise of salvation through Christ, the help of the Holy Spirit, and the fruit of a life that glorifies God. What could be better than that?

~

1. What do you think prompted Lloyd Harper to pursue a loan in spite of so many obstacles?

_____

_____

_____

_____

2. Why do you think Mr. Blackburn went to such lengths to approve a loan for an African-American with little to no collateral?

_____

_____

_____

_____

3. Have you been challenged to extend grace in a difficult situation like Mr. Blackburn did? How did you respond?

_____

_____

_____

_____

4. *How has someone else's kindness impacted your life?*

_____

_____

_____

_____

5. *With what gifts has God entrusted you? How can you use those gifts to serve your church or your community?*

_____

_____

_____

_____

CHAPTER TWO

REFLECTING CHRIST

Our chief responsibility as believers in Christ is to reflect His character to the world. Our thoughts, actions, and attitudes should all point back to Jesus, no matter what our circumstance. My parents taught me this truth by example. The manner in which they lived their lives and instructed their children was patterned after Scripture, and they were role models of everything a young man would want to see. They consistently exemplified the same values at home during the week as they did on Sundays at church.

My dad, Lloyd Harper, Sr., was born in Perry County in 1903. He was the fourth of twelve children born to Lee and Emily Harper. My mom, Walter Mae Whitehead, was born in 1906; there were twelve children in her family as well. You may wonder why a girl was given what is traditionally a boy's name. The reason is that my grandfather's favorite uncle was named Walter, and my grandparents had planned from the beginning to name their firstborn after him. When their firstborn turned out to be a girl instead of a boy, they chose to use the name anyway but added "Mae" to make it more suitable.

I do not know the details of Mom and Dad's first meeting, but I do know it was probably at church. Most socializing in that time was done at church or church-hosted functions. The local church was probably the most influential institution for the African-American population of any smaller Southern town. Every African-American in our area attended church regularly. It was a place to freely come together in safety and autonomy. It was where we learned not only spiritual truths but also public information so that we could all be well-informed citizens. In short, the church was the hub of the community.

Mom was fifteen or sixteen when she and Dad met. I'm sure Dad was interested from the first time he saw her, because Mom was always an attractive woman. She was about five and a half feet tall with "a little meat on her bones," as was common for African-American women of that time. No skinny model would have survived on a farm; you had to have some substance to do that kind of work.

Dad was around nineteen at the time he and Mom

met and was no less good-looking than Mom. Dad was about six feet tall and in very good shape. He presented a strong, capable image that Mom no doubt found appealing.

The two hit it off from the start and soon started going together. Dating in those days did not mean going out to restaurants or seeing shows; instead, young couples spent time together under the supervision of their families and the community. Most of my parents' "dates" were just the time they spent talking before or after church. Dad would also have visited Mom at her home and spent time in the company of her family.

Knowing their personalities, I have no doubt that Mom was the pursuer in that relationship. I'm not sure at what point it happened, but, one day, Mom looked at Dad and said to herself that he was the one. From then on, it was just a matter of time. I remember Mom telling one particular story from when they were dating. One afternoon, she and Dad had gone on a picnic, and Mom reached for him. At first Dad thought she was being fresh, but instead she grabbed his favorite piece of chicken. As Mom liked to put it, "Thank goodness, he married me anyway!"

My parents only dated for about a year. It was

common for folks to marry young in those days; with no circumstances or social conventions to delay them, there was really no reason for a young couple to wait once they had made up their minds to marry. My parents were wed in 1923 in Marion, Alabama. They had a very simple church wedding, which was also common in those days. Couples didn't spend crazy amounts of money on decorations and food, partly because there was no money for such expensive stuff and partly because things like that weren't seen as necessary. Mom and Dad celebrated in the style of the day, with fried chicken and cakes and pies for the guests.

Although my parents (especially my father) did not often demonstrate their affection physically or verbally, I know that they loved each other very much. As I got older, I learned to recognize the subtle ways in which they expressed their love. There was a comfortable sweetness about the way they interacted that made their devotion clear.

In order to have the best possible marriage, both husband and wife need to be unwaveringly committed not only to each other but, first and foremost, to serving the Lord Jesus Christ. That mutual commitment to Christ is what I believe held my parents' marriage together for forty-one years. Despite their different personalities, Mom and Dad had the most important thing in common: My parents gave God first place in everything they did.

~

When I think of my dad, Psalm 1 immediately comes to mind, particularly the first two verses: "Blessed is the man who walks not in the counsel of the wicked, nor stands in the way of sinners, nor sits in the seat of scoffers; but his delight is in the law of the Lord, and on his law he meditates day and night." The Hebrew word 'aš•rê (translated "blessed") is a word that describes celebration or enrichment; thus, a life willingly and wholeheartedly focused on God and His teaching is highly desirable not only for its own sake but for our happiness as well.

Dad certainly did get a great deal of happiness from serving the Lord through his life's work. His passion for farming was only outdone by his passion for the Lord. Because of that passion, the metaphor that the psalmist uses in verse 3 to describe a righteous man is especially fitting to describe my dad: "He is like a tree planted by streams of water that yields its fruit in its season, and its leaf does not wither. In all that he does, he prospers."

As a farmer, my dad went to work every day; you can't take sick leave when there are ten cows needing to be milked or several acres needing to be plowed or equipment needing to be repaired. Even when we weren't in the midst of a growing season, there were still plenty of things to do around the farm. Dad never shied away from hard work. On the contrary, taking care of the farm was what he considered fun. He was grateful to God to have some of the best farmland in Perry County and genuinely enjoyed working the ground. I remember one time when my dad was telling someone about his work on the farm that he commented, "I got the best job in the world because, while I'm sleeping, God is growing up the crop."

I know how much the farm meant to Dad, mostly because I could see it in his actions. Dad didn't say much about his feelings; in fact, he really didn't talk much at all. Dad was sober-minded and quiet. He was certainly not a jokester, although he did enjoy a good laugh. The only situations in which I ever saw him have extended conversations were with his customers when we were out selling vegetables. In those circumstances, he looked at all men as equals and spoke to them as friends. It did not matter whether they were the same race as him or not; Dad treated everyone fairly.

The Lord promises in Isaiah 58:11 that He "will guide you continually and satisfy your desire in scorched places and make your bones strong; and you shall be like a watered garden, like a spring of water whose waters do not fail." Dad was sustained by streams of living water through every season of life. I am sure that he encountered many difficulties along the way, a few of which I will recount later, but he remained faithful and brought forth not only literal fruit but also the spiritual fruit of a godly life.

My dad derived great happiness from serving the Lord through his life's work, farming.

My mom, in many ways, was the opposite of my dad. Whereas Dad was reserved and meek, Mom was outspoken and sassy. Dad was pretty much only interested in the farm, while Mom's interests were a bit more diverse. One aspect of Mom's life that highlights her personality well is how she watched her favorite soap opera. Mom was an avid fan of "As the World Turns," and somehow, even with everything she had to do in a day, she managed to never miss an episode. Mom would settle down in front of our family's only television and perhaps ask one of us kids to adjust the "rabbit ears" (antenna) to get a clearer picture. It was not uncommon for Mom to talk to the characters on the show as if they were real people in the room with her. I can recall one day, when one of the villains was doing something Mom especially didn't like, she grew heated and shouted, "I wish I could go through that television and grab you by the collar!"

The strength of Mom's personality was only outdone by her strength of character. The description of the virtuous woman in Proverbs 31 has always reminded me of my mom, because the wife in the passage is equally faithful and capable. She is strong without being overbearing, confident without being full of herself.

One of the ways that confidence is expressed is

through the wife's decisiveness. Verse 17 says that she "dresses herself with strength and makes her arms strong," indicating that she possesses both physical and spiritual fortitude. In other words, she is anything but a pushover. Mom was the same way. She was not one to beat around the bush about anything. She let us know if she didn't like something we were doing, but she usually had good reason for not liking it. Mom acted according to her convictions and stood by her decisions.

Like the wife of noble character, Mom demonstrated wisdom in everything she did. She had "mother wit," as they used to say in the South. Mom always could anticipate problems so well that at times we thought she could read our minds. In actuality, Mom was just very good at being prepared for any situation. She kept stock of all the family's resources to make sure we were never left wanting. My mom was an excellent cook and canner. She made sure nothing went to waste and canned food for the family to consume during the winter. This kind of readiness brings to mind the description of the virtuous wife in Proverbs 31:21: "She is not afraid of snow for her household, for all her household are clothed in scarlet."

Probably the most reiterated characteristic of the Proverbs 31 woman is her industriousness. There are descriptions throughout the passage of the work she does as a businesswoman, as a household manager, and as a mother. It is evident that she puts the needs of others first when prioritizing her to-do list: "She rises while it is yet night and provides food for her household and portions for her maidens" (31:15); and she perceives her efforts as valuable, not wasting them on fruitless ventures: "She looks well to the ways of her household and does not eat the bread of idleness" (31:27). Although Mom's daily tasks differed from those of biblical times, she demonstrated the same attitudes of selflessness and conscientiousness in her labor.

Just as Dad never took a day off from farm work as long as he was able, Mom never took a day off from taking care of the family. As I already mentioned, she was responsible for all of the household chores in addition to binding up scrapes, preparing lunches, mending clothes, and otherwise seeing to the needs of her children. Moreover, she did not shy away from extra work when something additional was needed. Between 1955 and 1960, our family's finances were a little thin, so Mom took a job to supplement our funds. She worked at the Marion Hospital as an orderly on the third shift, from 11 p.m. to 7 a.m. She would work all night and get off in the morning, but she would still have a family to cook and clean for when she got home. When she slept, I don't know.

From the context, it seems that the Proverbs wife of noble character was not required by her situation to do physical labor; she had handmaidens and presumably other servants in her household who could take care of such things. With that said, the fact that she takes on tasks such as spinning, sewing, and even farming indicates that she must find the labor gratifying in some way. She works intentionally rather than reluctantly. Although most of the work my mom did was because of necessity, she also got a good deal of personal satisfaction from a job well done.

Mom taught us to look for the same satisfaction in our own work. She heartily believed in doing something right the first time rather than doing it over. I saw the value of that strategy demonstrated in Mom's life, and, as I will explain later, I applied it to my career and ministry with great effect.

Besides personal satisfaction, Mom also received the gratitude and respect of her family as reward for her efforts. Although I'm sure we never thanked her enough for all she did for us through the years (how do you adequately thank someone for devoting her entire life to your benefit?), we did try to follow the example of Proverbs 31:28: "Her children rise up and call her blessed; her husband also, and he praises her."

Mom's influence went beyond the bounds of the Harper family; she also had a significant impact on our community at the time. Her biggest role outside our family was as a leader in our church. She was the wife of a deacon and had specific responsibilities associated with that. Mom planned most of the anniversary celebrations, homecoming events, and weekly services for our church. Her natural leadership abilities were highlighted in such circumstances, as she organized details and directed people to see to different tasks.

Mom would also organize quilting parties at our home in the winter. Four or five women would come together during the day (while we kids were at school) to make a quilt from start to finish. They chatted and worshipped together while they worked on piecing and sewing the quilts. A contraption of wooden rails that was hung from the ceiling provided the means for all the women to work on the quilt at the same time. These gatherings allowed the women of the community to minster to each other. They would help one another with quilting techniques and would cook dinner together so that the job did not fall to anyone on her own.

Mom was the life of the party when the ladies got together. She not only provided the forum for these women to serve each other by hosting the quilting parties at our house, but she also kept everyone on task so that they could enjoy the fruit of their labor at the end.

The time and effort Mom put into serving the community did not go unnoticed, nor did it go unappreciated. The people of the church were happy to have someone so capable at the helm to make sure that bigger events went smoothly, and the women who came to our home were grateful to be given a chance to enjoy time together. Proverbs 31:31 says, "Give her of the fruit of her hands, and let her works praise her in the gates." In other words, the virtuous wife is not praised as a matter of course; the good things that are said of her are deserved. The same is true of my mom. Any kind words spoken to Mom then or about her now are apt. The fruit of her life is a wonderful legacy of love.

~

When speaking of the qualities of my parents, it is as important to appreciate the integrity of their union as it is to appreciate their integrity as individuals. Within the passage about the virtuous wife is a description of what a marriage founded on faith and fueled by love would look like: "The heart of her husband trusts in her, and he will have no lack of gain. She does him good, and not harm, all the days of her life" (Proverbs 31:11-12).

Much of Dad's success as a businessman was indeed made possible by Mom's support. In addition to working alongside him in the cotton fields, she saw to the upkeep of the house, the preparation of meals, and the care of us children. Mom also held the role of treasurer in our home. I am sure we had a checking account at the Marion Bank and Trust Company, but we did not go to town often to cash a check; she always had the money the family needed. Dad would give the ultimate okay to spend anything, but Mom was the one who scrutinized each request for funds from the children.

Because Mom took care of all the extraneous tasks, Dad could focus on making our farm flourish. Dad, like the husband in the passage, knew he could trust the management of the household to Mom because she had proven herself on many occasions to be sensible and capable. It is evident that Dad trusted Mom's wisdom and discretion as well, because he spoke openly with her when he would not speak openly with anyone else. Mom was the only person with whom Dad would discuss matters of business or personal concern — or almost anything else, for that matter. Most of what I know about Dad's background was what he told to Mom and what she then related to us; Mom never seemed to mind being Dad's storyteller, though.

People noticed the love my parents had for each other and admired them for it. Mom and Dad never had a reputation for "running around" on each other. They remained faithful to the Lord and to each other as long as they lived, which was rare for African-American couples in that time. The people who came in contact with my parents respected their constancy and still talk about that today.

The faithfulness Mom and Dad showed to each other resembled the faithfulness that God shows to His people. As the Lord said to the prophet Jeremiah, "... I have loved you with an everlasting love; therefore I have continued my faithfulness to you" (Jeremiah 31:3). In many ways, a godly marriage is meant to resemble the relationship the Lord has with His followers. In Ephesians 5, the roles of husband and wife are used to illustrate how Christ relates to His Church.

First listed is the role of the wife, equated with the Church as a whole: "Wives, submit to your own husbands, as to the Lord. For the husband is the head of the wife even as Christ is the head of the church, his body, and is himself its Savior. Now as the church submits to Christ, so also wives should submit in everything to their husbands" (verses 22-24).

Wives are directed to "submit," a term that many modern thinkers find troublesome at best. It is important to look at the word in context, however: Wives are to submit in the same manner that the Church submits to Christ. The Church as a whole looks to Christ with reverence and respect. We seek to honor Him out of gratitude for all He has done for us. Because of His great love for us, we lovingly strive to please Him. So it is in a Christian marriage. A wife should submit to her husband not out of fear or obligation, but out of love and respect. The Church yields to the authority of Christ because we know we can trust Him with the whole of our lives. Similarly, a wife can feel secure going along with her husband's decisions when she expects that he has her best interests in mind.

This expectation is not unfounded if the husband is also following the biblical model of marriage. Husbands are charged with the responsibility of being worthy of their wives' respect: "Husbands, love your wives, as Christ loved the church and gave himself up for her, that he might sanctify her [...]. In the same way husbands should love their wives as their own bodies. He who loves his wife loves himself. For no one ever hated his own flesh, but nourishes and cherishes it, just as Christ does the church, because we are members of his body" (verses 25-29).

According to this passage, the two main responsibilities of a husband to his wife are to take care of her and to put her needs first. Jesus put our need of salvation before any rights He had as part of the Holy Trinity, temporarily trading the splendors of heaven for the confinement of a mortal body and suffering an undeserved death for the sake of His beloved creation. Since Christ's sacrifice is the standard by which love is gauged, clearly a husband's responsibility goes beyond simply buying a bouquet for an anniversary. He is to care for his wife as he does his own body — protecting her from injury of any kind, making sure she is satisfied both physically and emotionally, and finding healing if there is hurt.

The essence of the commandments to both husband and wife is that their love for each other must outweigh their love for themselves or for any other except God.

When both members of a couple are elevating the other above themselves, it results in good for the whole family — just as when the members of Christ's Church are responding to His amazing grace with intense devotion, it results in good for the Church as a whole.

I was blessed to have a godly model of marriage in my parents, and I have been blessed to be married to a godly woman for almost fifty years. Even if you don't have an earthly example of Spirit-fueled love, we all have the example of our heavenly Father's love. God has already chosen and vowed to be united with us for all eternity: "And I will betroth you to me forever. I will betroth you to me in righteousness and in justice, in steadfast love and in mercy. I will betroth you to me in faithfulness. And you shall know the Lord" (Hosea 2:19-20). He is the perfect "lover of our souls," never failing to be worthy of our trust and always loving limitlessly.

~

1. What does it mean to you to "delight" in the law of the Lord?

_____

_____

_____

_____

2. Isaiah 58:11 says that God will sustain us "like a well-watered garden"; and, likely referring to this passage, Jesus said that His followers would have "rivers of living water" flowing from their hearts. How has God sustained you in one of life's deserts? How can you "pour out" God's love onto others?

_____

_____

_____

_____

3. How can finding satisfaction in your work glorify God?

_____

_____

_____

_____

4. *What do you think were the lasting effects that Walter Mae Harper, a true Proverbs 31 woman, had on her community?*

_____

_____

_____

_____

5. *Lloyd and Walter Mae Harper demonstrated their love by putting each other's needs before their own. Do you know anyone who has demonstrated godly love in this way?*

_____

_____

_____

_____

CHAPTER THREE

LIVING UP TO THE LEGACY

The Harper family as a whole consisted of my parents, Lloyd and Walter Mae, and their twelve children: Josephine, Lloyd Junior, Eddie, Herbert, Jefferson Davis, Linzie, Alyce, Ruth, Eleanor, Richard, Robert, and myself. There was also a stillborn child that came between Ruth and Ellie, but the child was not named as far as I know. All the kids were born at home on the farm, with two or three years between each of us; so by the time the younger ones like myself came along, the older kids were already out in the workforce, serving in the military, or studying in college. There were probably never more than six or seven of us at home at any one time.

Having that many of us did make it easy to put together games like hide-and-go-seek or baseball, but I didn't mind as the number of kids in the house gradually became fewer. The only time I really wished there were more siblings around the house was when it came to doing chores. In general, the girls helped Mom around the house, while the boys worked outside with Dad. I thought the girls got off easy, but they tell it differently.

Growing up in a big family helped me to better understand what it means to be part of the Church, both in a local fellowship and in the global Christian community. I can see parallels between the ways my siblings and I related to each other and our parents and the ways believers relate to each other and to God. We children worked and enjoyed life together under the

My siblings and I gathered in 1964 for my dad's funeral. Back row, from left: Ruth, Linzie, Alyce, Ellie, Mom, Josephine. Front row: Robert, J.D., myself, Lloyd Junior, Eddie, and Richard.

authority of our parents, just as the Church works and worships together under the authority of Jesus Christ. Just as my siblings and I influenced each other as we grew in the likeness of our parents, so the children of God can influence one another as we grow in the image of God.

Unity

Unity among believers is one of the most important elements of the Christian life. Being unified in Christ means that we are placing our identity as children of God before all other interests. It means that, regardless of worship style or dress code, all who believe that Jesus died to pay the penalty for our sins and have entrusted Him with their lives are members of the same body and must function together for the good of the whole. This does not mean that all believers must agree on every detail of religious practice. Just as my siblings and I have various interests yet still all belong to the family of Lloyd and Walter Mae Harper, so Christians who pursue a relationship with Jesus in different ways are still all children of God.

Of course, where there are differences, there is likely

to be some friction. My siblings and I certainly didn't get along at all times, but in the end (sometimes with a little encouragement from Dad's belt), we always came to the conclusion that loving each other as family was more important than having our way. It is evident from the writings of Paul that the early believers struggled with remaining unified at times as well. That is why he urged them in Ephesians 4:1-3 "to live a life worthy of the calling you have received. Be completely humble and gentle; be patient, bearing with one another in love. Make every effort to keep the unity of the Spirit through the bond of peace" (NIV).

As Paul indicated, unity among believers mirrors the nature of God. Jesus prayed to the Father in the Garden of Gethsemane that his followers would become one, just as He and the Father are one, "so that the world may know that you sent me and loved them even as you loved me" (John 17:23). The three members of the Holy Trinity — Father, Son, and Holy Spirit — are of one mind; God cannot disagree with Himself. By not dwelling on differences between sects but coming together on the fundamentals of faith, we are demonstrating to the world the attributes of the God we serve. Theologian Francis Schaeffer observed the value of oneness among members of the Christian Church in his book *The Mark of the Christian*: "It is in the midst of a difference that we have our golden opportunity. When everything is going well and we are all standing around in a nice little circle, there is not much to be seen by the world. But when we come to the place where there is a real difference and we exhibit uncompromised principles but at the same time observable love, then there is something that the world can see, something they can use to judge that these really are Christians, and that Jesus has indeed been sent by the Father."[1]

Not only can believers testify to the unique love of God through their cooperation, they can also build up the body from within by working together. Romans 14:17-18 says, "For the kingdom of God is not a matter of eating and drinking but of righteousness and peace and joy in the Holy Spirit. Whoever thus serves Christ is acceptable to God and approved by men. So then let us pursue what makes for peace and for mutual upbuilding." We should not let petty arguments get in the way of loving each other as brothers and sisters in Christ. Members of the Church are to help each other and care for each other. That is the mark of a good family.

Accountability

In the Harper family, there was an expectation that the older children would carry out the responsibilities of the parents if Mom and Dad happened not to be around. My siblings and I weren't allowed to discipline each other, but you knew if an older brother or sister told you to do something, you'd better do it. The same is true in the family of God. Although we are never out of the sight of our heavenly Father, He still asks His children to be mindful of each other. It is not the responsibility of any of us to judge one another, but we are commanded to hold each other accountable to the standards set before us in Scripture. Paul talked about the responsibility we have to one another in Galatians 6:1-2: "Brothers, if anyone is caught in any transgression, you who are spiritual should restore him in a spirit of gentleness. Keep watch on yourself, lest you too be tempted. Bear one another's burdens, and so fulfill the law of Christ."

Now, it is important to note the approach that Paul advocates should be taken to bring Christians back to the fold. First of all, he specifies that it is only a brother who is *caught* in transgression — not just suspected or accused — that we should confront about wrongdoing. Moreover, the admonition should be presented in a spirit of gentleness (as opposed to a spirit of condemnation), which is fueled and guided by the Holy Spirit. We should speak with humility, knowing that our righteousness is in Christ alone and that, apart from His grace, we could be tempted to transgress in the same manner as our brother. We should also be supportive, emphasizing a desire to bring the erring child back into the fellowship of the family of God rather than rejecting him for his error and pushing him away.

It may not be politically correct for one man to "mind another's business," so to speak, but it is sometimes necessary to confront a brother about a behavior or attitude that is not in keeping with a child of God because the behavior of one person who bears the name of Christ affects the world's perception of all who bear the name of Christ. Parents are often evaluated by the behavior of their children. How many of us, if we encountered a toddler using profanity, wouldn't give the child's mother a questioning look? There are millions of people in this world who know Jesus by name only, and their only association with His name is the behavior of His followers. As the Apostle Paul pointed out, this means that "we are ambassadors for Christ, God making his appeal through us." What assumptions will people make about our heavenly Father based on our conduct?

The task of keeping one another accountable in a godly manner is not an easy one, and many of us would rather keep to ourselves rather than potentially cause tension, but we must remember that it is biblically mandated for believers to care for one another in this way. Not only that, but the potential benefits of speaking truth far outweigh any risk of awkwardness or embarrassment. To step in with a word of wisdom when a brother is struggling is to be a catalyst in the restoration of his relationship with God. In the words of James 5:19-20, "My brothers, if anyone among you wanders from the truth and someone brings him back, let him know that whoever brings back a sinner from his wandering will save his soul from death and will cover a multitude of sins."

Encouragement

It is our responsibility as believers not only to correct one another but also to protect one another. By reminding one another of the hope we have in Jesus Christ and demonstrating spiritual fortitude in our own lives, it may be possible to prevent a brother from falling away from the faith. Hebrews 3:13 tells us to "exhort one another every day, as long as it is called 'today,' that none of you may be hardened by the deceitfulness of sin." On our own, we are susceptible to faulty reasoning and overpowering emotions. Sometimes all we need is to hear truth spoken from a Christian brother or sister in order to renew our minds.

In that moment, when we are speaking love into someone's life, the spiritual needs of the other person must take priority. Sincere encouragement cannot come from a selfish heart. As Paul instructed in Philippians 2:3-4: "Do nothing from selfish ambition or conceit, but in humility count others more significant than yourselves. Let each of you look not only to his own interests, but also to the interests of others." By focusing primarily on our own struggles, we may miss seeing that a brother or sister is in need. On the other hand, by looking after others before ourselves, we may find more opportunities than expected to touch the lives of others.

Just as words of admonition must be chosen with wisdom, so words of encouragement must also be thoughtfully spoken. There is a godly manner of encouragement, which maintains proper perspective of who we are in Christ, and there is a worldly manner of encouragement, which blindly supports any endeavor. Colossians 3:16 tells believers to "let the word of Christ dwell in you richly, teaching and admonishing one another in all wisdom." As nice as it is to hear that I am special or talented, sometimes what I really need to get through a difficult situation is to hear that God is greater, that it is His purpose I am working towards and not my own.

Hebrews 10:24 says, "And let us consider how to stir up one another to love and good works." The word "consider" indicates that it may not be immediately obvious how to reach out to those around us, and not every person receives encouragement in the same way. Some need a great deal of prayer and a few aptly chosen words from a mentor. Others need to talk through their struggles with a friend and to hear truth within a larger conversation. In any case, the key to effectively helping one another is showing that you genuinely care.

The strength of your immediate spiritual family can greatly affect the strength of your personal walk with Christ. If the believers with whom you are in regular contact are active in their faith, then they are likely to encourage you to be more active in yours, as well. On the other hand, if the believers around you take a more passive approach to Christianity, then their lack of enthusiasm for God's work will likely rub off on you. Keep in mind that this goes both ways — if you yourself are somewhat lackadaisical in your Christian service, you may unconsciously be drawing those around you into a similar mindset. To see a ready example of how our family can influence us, look no further than the two brothers who were closest to me in age.

My brother Richard was a wild, fun-loving boy. If there was a way to get in trouble, he found it. He was often found playing instead of working, and he was good

My brothers Richard (center) and Robert (right) always had time to spend with me, their baby brother.

at encouraging me to join him in horsing around. My parents often held Richard responsible for our shenanigans because he was oldest of the group; I think they expected him to keep Robert and me in line, but Richard was much better at keeping things fun.

I remember one time when Richard tried to put one over on Mom. Mom fixed lunch every day for us to take to school, and one day she had fixed a cake to add as a special treat. Just as everyone was getting ready to leave for school, Mom became suddenly worried that she hadn't put cake in one bag. Richard piped up and said, "Mama, you must have forgotten to put it in my bag."

When it came down to Mom checking each of the lunch bags, Richard didn't want her to look in his bag. Of course, she did, and, of course, she found that he already had a piece of cake inside. Richard did end up getting one thing he hadn't bargained for that morning — a good old-fashioned spanking by Dad.

As mischievous as Richard was, my brother Robert was equally well-behaved. He tried to set a good example of dependability for Richard and me, which we sometimes followed. When he was a young man, Robert enjoyed working with his hands. He was very industrious and skilled in his work — qualities that he often used to fix the messes his brothers caused.

Robert was always ready to help Dad, and Dad trusted Robert to do a quality job on any assignment. Between the three of us, we knew that Dad counted on Robert more than he did on Richard or me. Whether the task was fixing a fence or plowing a section of field, Dad would usually put Robert in charge because he never had to worry about whether Robert was going to complete an assignment on time.

Seeing how Dad depended on Robert and promoted him to a position of leadership motivated me to be more

My brother Robert shows off one of Dad's prized melons, while I hold my niece, Sharon. Mom and my sister Ruth are in the swing, and my sister Linzie is behind me.

like Robert, both in the way he responded to Dad's instructions and the way he handled himself in general. Robert always showed that he wanted to do things the right way, and that made me want to follow his example.

A verse often quoted in regards to the interdependence of believers is Proverbs 27:17: "Iron sharpens iron, and one man sharpens another." To say that we are to build each other up is not to say that some members of the church are more valuable than others or that one has authority over another. We are all iron, so to speak — equally fallible but equally forgiven. Knowing that we are to strengthen others in the faith encourages us to stay strong ourselves. We all have the same ultimate goal, which is to glorify God with every aspect of our lives. If we ourselves are pursuing that goal and simultaneously encouraging others to do so, then God is glorified all the more.

Emulation

We can build up one another with words, but we can also teach and learn by example. This is true in the family of God, and it was equally true in the Harper family. My sister Eleanor was one of the siblings whose example influenced me most. Of all the kids, she probably made the most effort to be close to Mom and Dad. As I mentioned before, Dad wasn't the kind of man who liked to open up, but she certainly encouraged him to do so. Eleanor was always very studious and thrived on the praise she received from our parents for reaching and surpassing goals in her schoolwork. Although neither of my parents were great scholars, they taught by example the importance of a good work ethic and the value of pursuing excellence to the glory of God. Eleanor followed their example as it applied to her studies, and I in turn learned from Eleanor how rewarding academic success could be.

My brother Robert also had a profound influence on my school career. Not only was Robert an accomplished scholar, but he was a talented athlete as well; he was certainly an exception to the stereotype of "dumb jocks." Robert showed me that a person can excel in more than one field, and his example encouraged me to pursue excellence in all of my endeavors. Robert was my hero growing up — I wanted to be just like him. My parents were the source of wisdom for both Robert and Eleanor, but seeing how my sister and brother behaved in response to their teaching reinforced the lesson for me.

Hebrews 13:7 tells believers to "remember your leaders, those who spoke to you the word of God. Consider the outcome of their way of life, and imitate their faith." Christians today are blessed to have over two thousand years of role models and writing to show us what a life dedicated to the Lord should look like. These include martyrs and heroes of the faith such as William Tyndale and D.L. Moody; they also include, for many of us, examples closer to home such as parents, pastors, and Sunday school teachers.

All the children in the Harper family learned from our parents' example and grew up with a desire to glorify God in every aspect of our lives. Like our parents, God has honored our desire to serve Him, causing us to excel in our respective vocations. Robert earned his bachelor's degree in business administration and became the successful manager of a certified public accounting firm. Eleanor earned her master's degree in public health and has had a successful career in medical research. Linzie, Ruth, and Alyce became registered nurses, and Linzie earned a master's degree as a clinical nurse specialist. Lloyd Junior became a successful master mechanic in Birmingham. Jefferson Davis and Eddie built careers as factory workers. Josephine worked in housekeeping for the Veterans Administration. The baby of the family became the vice president of human resources in a Fortune 100 company. Even Richard eventually got his act together. A stint in the Air Force helped Richard to mature and prepared him for a successful career as a Los Angeles police officer. After working the beat for almost twenty years, Richard went on to become the owner of two McDonald's restaurants.

Now that the children of Lloyd and Walter Mae Harper are grown up and have children of our own, it is our responsibility to be that example of faith to the next generation. Whether or not we are actively instructing our children and grandchildren, we should be teaching them how to walk in righteousness by showing them how it is done. For every brother or sister in the family of

The passage of time can't diminish the closeness between brothers. My brother Richard and I enjoy a moment together at Mom's house in the mid-1970s.

God, there is a younger sibling who needs the example of the previous generation to help him along the way. Peter knew the importance of the role of mature believers in the family of God and charged them with the care of the younger ones: "So I exhort the elders among you, as a fellow elder and a witness of the sufferings of Christ, as well as a partaker in the glory that is going to be revealed: shepherd the flock of God that is among you, exercising oversight, not under compulsion, but willingly, as God would have you" (1 Peter 5:1-2). You never know who might be looking to you for guidance, so be careful how you walk, and live a life that gives credit to God's family.

~

1. *John 1:12-13 says, "But to all who did receive him, who believed in his name, he gave the right to become children of God, who were born, not of blood nor of the will of the flesh nor of the will of man, but of God." What does it mean to you to be a child in the family of God?*

---

2. What do you think hinders Christians from getting along with their brothers and sisters in Christ? How can you pursue unity with other believers?

_____

_____

_____

_____

3. Why is accountability important in the family of God? Has there been a time in your life when a fellow believer put you back on track?

_____

_____

_____

_____

4. What are some ways that you can stir up others to love and good works?

_____

_____

_____

_____

5. *Ephesians 5:1 says, "Therefore be imitators of God, as beloved children." Who do you look to as an example of godly living? How can you be that example to someone around you?*

_____

_____

_____

_____

CHAPTER FOUR

THE VALUE OF A GOOD NAME

We know that one can have a great deal of influence on those who are in close contact with him, but can a godly life have an impact outside of one's friend group or church body? Absolutely! A person's reputation can inspire respect and admiration, even when only the barest details of that person's life are known.

Proverbs 22:1 says, "A good name is to be chosen rather than great riches, and favor is better than silver or gold." My parents didn't leave me much in the way of material goods, but they did leave the best thing they could have — a sterling reputation. They both conducted themselves in such a manner as to be above reproach in every circumstance. They were consistently honest, trustworthy, and kind, so that even those who had not met them face to face knew that Lloyd and Walter Mae Harper were people who could be counted on.

For my dad, farming was a full-time job. He was both laborer and manager, leading us and working alongside us every step of the way. In the spring, he would plow and lead us in planting ten acres of cotton (the federally mandated maximum); we hand-hoed the grass out until the cotton was ready to harvest, which could happen anytime from early September to late October. There was no revenue or profit between the time the cotton was planted in the spring until it was picked and sold in the fall, so my dad had to plan ahead in order to feed his family until the cotton came in. We planted other crops like corn, peas, collard greens, and turnips to sell in the meantime. Rather than setting up a roadside stand, my dad would load vegetables in his pickup truck and drive three delivery routes he had established around the towns of Greensboro, Uniontown, and Marion, Alabama.

We would pick vegetables on Mondays, Wednesdays and Fridays; on Tuesdays, we would visit homes in Greensboro; on Thursdays, we would drive through Uniontown; and on Saturdays, we would go to Marion. Dad had a specific route in each town, stopping at the homes of people with whom he had already established a business relationship. Even up into the 1950s and 1960s, it wasn't deemed acceptable for an African-American man to ring the front doorbell of a Caucasian person's home; instead, we would take our produce to the back door. After one of my brothers or I had knocked on the door, we'd say something such as, "Mrs. Smith, we are here selling vegetables and we have these to sell today. What would you like?"

Sometimes the lady of the house would come to the truck and look at the produce, while other times she would simply ask us for six pounds of peas or two watermelons or three cantaloupes or some of each. Most of the times, she would invite us in to place the produce on the counter and then pay us in cash. Dad never overstepped his boundaries when he went into the home of one of his customers, and he taught his sons to do the same thing. It would have been easy for any one of the mothers or young daughters whose homes we entered to claim that something inappropriate had taken place, but nothing ever happened in the many years that Dad had these routes. That is a tribute to the integrity of the man called Lloyd Harper, Sr.

Dad set out to delight his customers with the service and goods he provided. First of all, he always was courteous; he dressed properly and spoke in a kind manner. Furthermore, he was always generous and insisted that his customers get more than they paid for. If a woman ordered six pounds of peas, we always weighed out seven or eight pounds; if she asked for a dozen ears of corn, she would get fifteen. Our produce was always fresh, but if one of his customers complained about the quality of anything, my dad always replaced it twofold.

Dad not only gave more than he was asked, but he also asked very little in return. During the winter, Dad would go into the woods and hand-cut a cord of wood. He'd load it onto the truck so that it was brimming over, and then he'd go and unload it at the back door of a customer's house. For all that, he only charged four dollars. I would ask him, "Dad, why do you charge so little when you're working so hard?"

He'd reply, "I'm not trying to break anyone."

Dad was always generous with his service, and God honored Dad's generosity by making him successful. There were days in the late 1950s and early 1960s in which we sold over a hundred dollars' worth of vegetables, even while providing our customers with three pounds of peas for the price of two pounds and selling watermelons too big to carry for less than fifty cents.

Not only did Dad receive monetary rewards from his benevolent business practices, but he also reaped the benefits of his customers' loyalty and trust. Because he always dealt with people honestly and always gave more than he was asked, there were many of Dad's customers who would not buy vegetables from anyone but him. After Dad had taken our good-quality produce to a house a couple times, the customer learned to expect that kind of quality from our farm every time — and Dad did not disappoint.

Although it was certainly good business practice for Dad to be kind to his customers, that is not the primary reason he treated them so well. The caliber of Dad's character was revealed in the way that he treated everyone, not just the people who bought produce from him. Dad believed in "the golden rule," which is actually a divine command spoken by Jesus Christ: namely, that we should treat others as we would want to be treated (Luke 6:31). This simple life principle propelled Dad to interact respectfully with everyone, regardless of their age, gender, or race. He went out of his way to make sure that the people he dealt with felt appreciated, and they appreciated him in turn.

Undeserved Kindness

Of course, not everyone responded in kind to Dad's deferential manner. One day when we were "peddling"

vegetables in Marion, a Caucasian man drove his car
up next to Dad's window and told him to pull over.
Apparently the man thought Dad had pulled out in
front of him at a stop sign. This man was just another
citizen, not a police officer, but he spoke with the tone
of someone trying to put Dad in his place; the man
assumed, as many unfortunately did in that era, that he
was a better person than my dad simply because of the
color of his skin.

Dad did pull over, and the other man got out of his
car and came to Dad's window. As I watched from the
passenger seat, the man called Dad some terrible names
and accused Dad of trying to kill him with his truck. The
man ranted and raved for what seemed like an eternity
(although it was probably no more than five minutes),
but Dad never said a word the entire time. He kept his
hands on the steering wheel and his eyes straight ahead.
When the man finished his outburst, he simply got back
in his vehicle and drove off. Dad did not say a word to
me about what had just happened; he simply drove on to
the next house for us to sell vegetables.

My dad was as strong as an ox, and there is no doubt
in my mind that he could have physically whipped that
man and been justified in doing so; however, responding

in anger, even righteous anger, was not the right thing to do in that situation. Dad knew his job that day was to sell vegetables and get himself and me home safely, so he chose not to cause an incident that could have resulted in danger to both of us.

I mentioned before that Dad lived his life according to the "golden rule," a rule that is probably familiar to most people. What may not be as familiar is the context in which that verse appears. The command to treat others as well as we would want to be treated (which, if we are honest, is probably pretty well indeed) comes at the end of a passage about how to treat the least desirable people in our lives: "But I say to you who hear, love your enemies, do good to those who hate you, bless those who curse you, pray for those who abuse you. To one who strikes you on the cheek, offer the other also, and from one who takes away your cloak do not withhold your tunic either. Give to everyone who begs from you, and from one who takes away your goods do not demand them back" (Luke 6:27-30).

At first glance, this passage seems to advocate a position of weakness. To allow others to deal with us unkindly or unfairly is usually seen as pathetic, and to treat those who take advantage of us with love and generosity seems ridiculous; however, remember the example of Jesus Himself. In His death, Jesus demonstrated the kind of unconditional kindness He asks us to show others. After he had been beaten, mocked, pierced by thorns and nails, and hung on a cross to die, Jesus prayed for those who were killing Him, "Father, forgive them, for they know not what they do" (Luke 23:34).

Far from revealing weakness, a humble response requires great strength of spirit. Our natural reactions to pain, whether physical or emotional, are either to fight back or run away. What Jesus asks of us is neither of these options. He has instructed us to show forbearance, not giving others the reaction they deserve and giving them instead the kindness they do not deserve. We are to bravely face our assailants and offer the same grace to them that God offered us when we were His enemies.

The term "enemies" may seem strong, but consider this: The Oxford English Dictionary defines an enemy as "an unfriendly or hostile person." As much as Christians are privileged to call Jesus a friend once we have been saved, prior to that transformation we were not friendly to God. Our own hostility towards the One who made us and loves us far outweighs what most of us will ever experience, if for no other reason than that it is the willful rejection of a perfect being — He is incapable of deserving our rebuff.

Others may look down on us, but some of us have at one point denied that God even exists. Others may constantly ask us for favors, but some of us have and still do pray to God as if He were a vending machine to dispense answers to our requests. Others may disrespect and disregard you, but all of us are guilty at times of pursuing selfish interests instead of seeking first the kingdom. The beauty of the gospel is that we do not have to remain on unfriendly terms with God, "for if, while we were God's enemies, we were reconciled to him through the death of his Son, how much more, having been reconciled, shall we be saved through his life!" (Romans 5:10, NIV).

I never heard Dad talk about that day afterwards, not even to Mom, but the experience is one that has stayed with me. I remember his reaction whenever I encounter an injustice. What I learned from my dad that day is that the spiritual rewards that come from a humble heart far outweigh any loss — of dignity, or otherwise. All that bully gained from the confrontation was the momentary satisfaction of blowing off steam, and he came away looking foolish and immature. Dad won the respect and admiration of his son, and he preserved his reputation as a godly man.

Although turning the other cheek may cost us our pride, our well-being, or even our lives, still we would have lost nothing of real, eternal value. And since the things of God are what matter most, we have guaranteed victory in Him. As Paul (who suffered many indignities and injuries for the sake of the gospel) wrote in Romans 8:35 and 37: "Who shall separate us from the love of Christ? Shall tribulation, or distress, or persecution, or famine, or nakedness, or danger, or sword? [...] No, in all these things we are more than conquerors through him who loved us."

~

The beauty of a good reputation such as my dad had is that it is a reflection of the goodness of God. Most people knew that Dad was a Christian, so whenever he exemplified Christlike behavior, he brought glory to God as well as to himself. In the words of Richard Stearns, president of the international relief organization World Vision, "When we committed ourselves to following Christ, we also committed to living our lives in such a way that a watching world would catch a glimpse of God's character — His love, justice, and mercy — through our words, actions, and behavior."[1]

We may not have the opportunity to verbally share the Gospel with everyone we meet, but each of us has the opportunity to point to Christ through the evidence of a transformed life.

I return to my hometown every couple of years, and even now people will stop me and ask, "Are you Lloyd Harper's son?" When I tell them I am, they gladly share with me stories about the impact Dad's kindness had on their lives, testifying to his love for the Lord and the integrity of his character. These might be common conversation topics after a recent death, but Dad died more than fifty years ago.

When folks share stories about my dad, there is an unvoiced expectation that I will live up to the same standard as he did. You can pass on houses and money to your children, but the thing that has helped me the most, the thing that I believe is the most important, is a good name. Romans 12:1-2 says that God requires a living sacrifice. That doesn't mean we have to be perfect, but it does mean we should be living in a way that reflects God's standards.

One person on whom Dad's character had a profound

impact was Lee Benson, a young man who came to Marion at the age of twelve and only stayed until he graduated high school. He and I knew each other from the high school basketball team. Although his acquaintance with my dad was very brief, it was apparently very meaningful. A few years ago, although we hadn't kept up with each other since our school days, Lee contacted me to share a story about my dad. I've included Lee's letter here to show how large of an impact a godly man can have on those around him:

> *It was the year of 1964 and I was working as a male nurse's aide at the Perry County Hospital in Marion, Alabama. I was a seventeen-year-old student and a member of the Lincoln High School basketball team. A friend of mine, Don Harper, also attended Lincoln High School and was my teammate on the basketball team. Don had such a sweet spirit and was very easy to talk to. When I got to meet and know his family, I understood why he exhibited this Spirit of God in his personality. It was the same Spirit that was in his parents. Don and I played the same position on the basketball team for three years and became good friends.*

I admired him because he had something that I never had growing up — a functional father in his home.

The real impact that this family had on me was through the father, Mr. Lloyd Harper. Mr. Harper became ill and was admitted to Perry County Hospital. It was my job as a male nurse's aide to take care of the male patients, making sure that they had fresh water to drink and fresh bedding; I also helped them with meals and made sure that they were comfortable. During the two or three weeks that Mr. Harper was hospitalized, the concern and closeness his family displayed was unbelievable. I spent many, many hours with Mr. Harper and was in his room the day he died.

I can still remember that afternoon after Mr. Lloyd Harper died, when Don and his older brother Richard came to the hospital to visit their father, unaware that he had passed away. They seemed to be in good spirits as they entered what had been their father's room. They saw that his bed was rolled up, which was the procedure after a patient had died. Don and Richard ran out in the hallway. As I approached them, they both cried out, "Where is Daddy?"

I had to explain to them that their father had died about two hours earlier that day. The hurt on their faces was something that words cannot express. You could tell that a strong link in a family bond had been broken. I knew from that moment forward that if I ever had the privilege of having a family, my children would grow up with the love and support of their father being in their lives. I would be that strong bond in their lives, as Mr. Lloyd Harper had been to his family.

I graduated from Lincoln High School on May 27, 1965, and have never returned to Marion since then, but I still remember the experience I had with the Harper family and their father and the impact it had in shaping my life. I have been married for forty-five years and have five children, eleven grandchildren and two great grandchildren. I recently retired from Dayton Public Schools after twenty-eight years of service as a chemistry teacher. I tried to exhibit the same warmness and strong father image to my family and my students as I observed in Mr. Lloyd Harper with his family.

I have always believed that God puts great people in your life to help you to become the person that he wants you to be, and I thank him for granting me the blessing of the Harper family and this strong black man. Thank you, Mr. Lloyd Harper, for being a silent role model in my life. May God bless your soul. Your legacy continues to live on.

~

1. *Why do you think Lloyd Harper was so generous with his customers?*

_____

_____

_____

_____

2. *How was Lloyd Harper's life made better through his kindness?*

_____

_____

_____

_____

3. *Have you ever faced an injustice or an attack from an enemy? How did you respond? How should a believer respond?*

_____

_____

_____

_____

4. *What does it mean to you to read that we are "more than conquerors" in Christ?*

_____

_____

_____

_____

5. *Why do you think having a "good name" is so valuable?*

_____

_____

_____

_____

CHAPTER FIVE

REJOICING IN ALL THINGS

My family has been very blessed through the years, but make no mistake — things were not always pleasant or easy after my parents acquired the farm. Farming is, by nature, a risky business. There are a hundred and one things that can go wrong in a growing season. When you first get seeds put in the ground, there might be too much rain, such that the young plants are washed away before they mature; or there might not be enough rain, such that the plants grow stunted and weak. Even once the seedlings get bigger, there could be high winds that break down the stalks or insects that eat the leaves or extremely high temperatures that cause the plants to wither.

My parents did not even have the mechanized equipment that most farmers these days rely on, which would have made the jobs of breaking up the dirt and plowing furrows much less physically strenuous. Instead, everything was done by hand or by mule. Some jobs, like baling hay or dusting the cotton to prevent boll weevils from destroying the crop, required specialized equipment. For these, Dad would make arrangements for someone to come out with the necessary machinery and perform the task. We boys liked to stand out in the cotton field and watch while an airplane flew over to dust the plants with pesticides; it is a miracle that any of us lived to adulthood.

My parents were totally dependent on God to provide the right conditions for their crops to grow, and He was faithful to do it. They never lost an entire crop in all their years of farming; the worst that happened was that they needed to replant a few sections some years. The risk of losing everything was always there, but my parents never allowed the tenuousness of their situation to cause them fear or anxiousness; they trusted in the provision of their loving heavenly Father and had peace in their souls.

In Matthew 6:26-33, Jesus describes how God the Father loves and cares for His children:

> *Look at the birds of the air: they neither sow nor reap nor gather into barns, and yet your heavenly Father feeds them. Are you not of more value than they? [...] And why are you anxious about*

clothing? Consider the lilies of the field, how they grow: they neither toil nor spin, yet I tell you, even Solomon in all his glory was not arrayed like one of these. But if God so clothes the grass of the field, which today is alive and tomorrow is thrown into the oven, will he not much more clothe you, O you of little faith? Therefore do not be anxious, saying, "What shall we eat?" or "What shall we drink?" or "What shall we wear?" For the Gentiles seek after all these things, and your heavenly Father knows that you need them all. But seek first the kingdom of God and his righteousness, and all these things will be added to you.

My parents may never have had expensive wardrobes or grand furnishings, but we always had food on the table and clothing to wear. God may not provide everything we *want*, but He has promised to give us everything we *need*. The key to experiencing joy in every circumstance is recognizing God's grace in the midst of it.

When I was young, I didn't like farm work. It was hard and hot. We owned as many as eight milk cows at a time, and they had to be milked by Dad and us boys twice a day, seven days a week. We boys had to miss

two or three days of school a week between August
and October when it was time to pick the cotton, and
that was hard on a child like myself who was driven to
excel academically. Granted, I was on the honor roll all
throughout my school years and eventually graduated
in the top 1 percent of my class, but I still begrudged the
time spent away from my books.

Farm work was also just plain dirty. When relatives
came to visit from the city in their fancy cars, I always
felt self-conscious coming in from the fields all hot and
sweaty. One time, Mom asked me about running the
farm when I was grown up, and I said that I would only
choose to do it willingly if the alternative was getting put
in jail. She didn't like that too much.

I couldn't understand then how my dad could get so
excited about menial jobs around the farm. I have since
realized that Dad's enthusiasm didn't necessarily come
from the work itself; after all, milking cows in a cow lot
amidst all their droppings is hardly the most glamorous
job in the world. I don't think there was any level of work
that my dad thought was beneath him because it was
all part of taking care of the farm with which God had
blessed him.

As much as Dad saw divine purpose in even the

most mundane outdoor tasks, Mom saw the care of our family as her God-given work. I do not know how many hours of sleep she must have sacrificed over the years to make sure we were all clothed and fed and well, but you could tell she loved being a wife and mother.

Both my parents loved the Lord, and it showed in everything they did. They were never embarrassed about sharing that God was the reason for their blessing. Whether they were chopping cotton or plowing with a mule or digging potatoes, they found happiness in doing the work to which God had called them. It's hard to imagine rejoicing when you're spending long hours laboring under a hot sun, but my parents proved it was possible.

Mom and Dad would sing and pray together as they worked in the field, and people passing by would see them glorifying God in the midst of doing difficult work. Through this simple practice, my parents demonstrated the power of the gospel, and those who heard them may have been led to seek Christ because of my parents' living testimony. Mom and Dad's unconditional devotion to the Lord certainly had an effect on me. Many of the Scriptures that are meaningful to me today were quoted to me by parents in the field. Not only that, but their prayer and encouragement brought me through a personal struggle to the greatest joy I've ever known.

In southern African-American churches in the 1940s, you did not simply get up at the end of a service and walk to the front and tell the pastor you wanted to be baptized; if you were of age (ten years old or older) and wanted to give your heart to God, you were required to go through a period of prayer, testing, and revival on the "mourner's bench." The mourner's bench was a special seat at the front of the church for those who felt God was calling them into a relationship with His Son, Jesus. Most churches only held a revival once a year, so there was only a one-week period each year during which a new believer could be officially recognized by the church as a candidate for baptism.

On the bench, you listened intently to the preaching and prayers of the saints and waited until you heard a specific calling from God for you to accept His Son. The process itself was not what guaranteed the transformation of an unbeliever, but it was a tradition of the African-American church at the time.

In August of 1959, I told my parents that I wanted to be saved and was allowed to sit on the mourner's bench. I took my place and waited to hear from the Lord; however, by Thursday morning, I still had not received any specific "call." I struggled with self-doubt and was really worried that I would go through the entire week and not come off the mourner's bench, which would have been devastating for me and for my parents.

My mom saw me working in the yard that Thursday morning, and I guess she could tell I was troubled. She came right out to where I was working and asked me why I was struggling. I explained about not hearing the call of God. Mom then asked, point-blank, "Do you believe that Jesus came into the world to save you?"

I told her I did, and she replied, "Then just ask Him to come into your heart, and that will be enough."

I accepted Jesus Christ while standing in the farmyard with my mom, the Proverbs 31 mother and teacher, acting as the evangelist and asking the right questions. I went to church that evening for the revival and made my official profession of faith in front of the other church members. I was baptized in a pond near our church, and God has been transforming my life ever since.

~

True joy is not dependent on circumstances but is based in the unchanging nature of God Himself. As

John Piper writes, "Christian joy is a good feeling in the soul, produced by the Holy Spirit, as he causes us to see the beauty of Christ in the Word and in the world."

Most of us struggle at some time or another to have this "good feeling," but the important thing to remember is that the burden of producing joy does not lie within ourselves — joy is produced and sustained by the Holy Spirit.

The joy of the Lord enabled my parents to thrive despite the day-to-day struggles, and God's grace was sufficient to bring my family through tragedy as well. One of my brothers, Herbert, was born hydrocephalic; he was a "water head," as it was commonly called at that time. An abnormal buildup of fluid in his brain caused him to have many physical and mental disabilities and ultimately resulted in his death at the age of eleven. For those eleven years, Herbert was completely dependent on the rest of the family for his care.

Although I was not yet born when Herbert was around, I learned the details of that difficult time from my siblings. Herbert was not mobile, so any time he had to be moved, Mom or Dad would have to pick him up, sometimes with the help of one of the other children. We could not afford store-bought diapers, so Mom made cloth diapers and hand-washed them whenever necessary. For Herbert to eat, he had to be physically fed. Herbert could not be left alone, so one of the other children would stay at home with him while the rest of the family went to the field to work.

My mom was the primary caregiver for this young son. What amazes me is that, no matter how hard things got, Mom never complained. She continued loving and serving all of us even when she must have felt frustrated or exhausted. Her contentment was consistent because it was rooted in the peace of the Holy Spirit.

When Herbert died, Mom grieved for her child but did not despair. Underneath the sadness, she trusted that God had a purpose in giving her a little boy with such great needs and then taking him from her at such a young age. She was comforted in the knowledge that Herbert was suffering from his disabilities no longer but was safe in the arms of the Lord, and that she would be reunited with her son when she too left this world.

Psalm 37:23-24 says, "The steps of a man are established by the Lord, when he delights in his way; though he fall, he shall not be cast headlong, for the Lord upholds his hand." This verse tells us that we are never out of God's care and compassion. He knows our path before we set out on it and helps us along the way. Imagine a child just learning to walk, and the parent holding his hands and walking beside him to show him the way. That is the idea behind this verse. There is something beautiful in that image, of God reaching out His hand to grasp the hand of His child and pulling His child up to walk beside Him once more.

Christian joy is rooted in hope, which is rooted in God Himself. In Romans 15:13, Paul prayed, "May the God of hope fill you with all joy and peace in believing, so that by the power of the Holy Spirit you may abound in hope." The important thing to note from this verse (and to keep in mind in trying circumstances) is that the feeling of joy is not one we must conjure up within ourselves through denial or willfulness; joy comes directly from the Lord and is sustained by His power. And rather than just enabling us to be "okay," God gives joy in abundance so that we are more than satisfied — we are filled.

Even when someone is brought to the throne of God in tears, once they have come in contact with the Holy One and seen this fleeting life through His eternal perspective, they will come away with a deep-set contentment that nothing can shake. Think of Paul and

Silas, who were imprisoned after freeing a young girl from an evil spirit. They were beaten with rods, taken into an inner prison, and locked by their feet into stocks (Acts 16:2-24). Rather than responding with anger towards their attackers or sadness in their surroundings, the Bible tells us that they were "praying and singing hymns to God" (Acts 16:25). They weren't putting on a show of faith for the guard or even ignoring their dire situation. Instead, they were seeing their present trouble as insignificant in comparison to the promise of eternal life with Christ. They were overcome with the joy of loving and being loved by the Creator of the universe.

Philippians 3:8 says, "Indeed, I count everything as loss because of the surpassing worth of knowing Christ Jesus my Lord." This doesn't mean devaluing good or necessary aspects of our earthly lives; instead, it means raising our estimation of a relationship with God. John Piper explains it this way: "Knowing Christ right now, experiencing fellowship with him right now, is more precious, more satisfying, more sweet than anything else. We are not just waiting to see how all the circumstances are going to turn out when he works everything for good. We are experiencing the sweetness in Christ right now in the moment."[2]

~

The very fact that God created us with the ability to experience joy is evidence of how much He loves us. We can feel wonder at the sight of the night sky, smile at the smell of a rose, or be satisfied in the taste of a delicious meal; and just as a parent would take pleasure in seeing a child gleefully play with a toy he had been given, our heavenly Father takes pleasure in the simple joy of His children when they are appreciating His gifts. In glorifying God, we are simply turning our joy from the object itself to the One who gave it to us. As Psalm 147:11 tells us, "The Lord takes pleasure in those who fear him, in those who hope in his steadfast love."

When we very much enjoy something, most of us have the urge to talk about it with whomever will listen; just think of how often newlyweds speak of their spouses, so enthralled are they with the newfound joy of sharing life together. In pondering this concept, C.S. Lewis noted that "all enjoyment spontaneously overflows into praise unless (sometimes even if) shyness or the fear of boring others is deliberately brought in to check it. [...] I had not noticed either that just as men spontaneously praise whatever they value, so they spontaneously urge us to join them in praising it."[3]

A good example of that tendency to urge others to praise can be found in my mom. As we her children grew up and began reaching milestones and achieving success in our various fields, we would always send updates to the Marion Times-Standard. This was not for our own sake, but for Mom's; one thing Mom always enjoyed doing was bragging on her children, and she loved to get calls on the party line from neighbors who had seen one of our names in the paper. It didn't matter whether our achievements were big or small; Mom would burst with pride to hear about all of them.

The joyful pride that Mom exhibited for her children is what we should be exhibiting for God each and every day. We should be excited by the work He is doing, pleased by any new message from Him, and in awe of who He is. Mom may have reacted to our small successes with an overabundance of adulation, but it is impossible to overpraise God — He is worthy of all our worship.

C.S. Lewis describes worship as the only way to properly respond when we behold God's glory, and uses the illustration of a painting to explain: "What do we mean when we say that a picture is 'admirable'? We certainly don't mean that it is admired, for bad work is admired by thousands and good work may be ignored. Nor that it 'deserves' admiration in the sense in which a candidate deserves a high mark from the examiners. [...] The sense in which a picture deserves or demands admiration is rather this: that admiration is the correct, adequate, or appropriate response to it; that, if paid, admiration will not be thrown away; and that, if we do not admire, [...] we shall have missed something."[4]

The Bible tells us in 1 Peter 2:9 that praising God is not only a right response to His attributes, but one of the purposes to which we have been called: "But you are a chosen people, a royal priesthood, a holy nation, God's special possession, that you may declare the praises of him who called you out of darkness into his wonderful light."

Worshipping the Lord allows us to simultaneously love Him, please Him, and obey Him, all of which bring our hearts into greater intimacy with His. Through one act, we can experience the sweetness of God's presence within us while proclaiming His magnitude and power and thereby furthering His kingdom. Now that is something for which we can be truly joyful!

~

1. How did Lloyd and Walter Mae Harper demonstrate their joy in the Lord?

_____

_____

_____

_____

2. How did that joy impact those around them?

_____

_____

_____

_____

3. What potential obstacles to joy did the Harper family experience? What obstacles have you experienced?

_____

_____

_____

_____

4. What enabled the Harper family to rejoice in difficult circumstances? How can we know true joy in every season of life?

_____

_____

_____

_____

5. How does joy grow our relationship with God?

_____

_____

_____

_____

CHAPTER SIX

LETTING THE JOY SPILL OVER

The same God-given joy that sustains us in times of need can spill over as God-given blessings to others. Sometimes God allows this to happen without our even realizing it; we may touch someone's life simply by living in the fullness of the Holy Spirit and reflecting that in our lifestyle and language. At other times, God asks us to be the feet of the gospel, ready to act in His name to demonstrate His love so that others may know Him better. The product of our love for God is a regard for others made in his image. Just as joy grows internally when we turn our focus from self to God, so His joy is spread to others when we sacrifice our will to that of the Lord and act in accordance with His love. My father demonstrated this kind of self-sacrificial love in a very practical way.

For my family and others in our area who farmed for a living, harvesting a healthy crop in the fall meant financial stability for the rest of the year. A farmer's livelihood would depend on his being able to get his seeds in the ground in due season. When I was a boy, most of the farmers in our area still used mules to pull heavy farm equipment; tractors had not yet become common. Most of the time you could plow with one mule, but other tasks required a two-mule team.

Dad owned two mules and a horse. He loved those three animals and treated them very well, since God had provided them to help him work the farm. One of our neighbors down the road had the misfortune of losing one of his mules just before the growing season. He was not in a position to replace the one that died, so he came to my dad for help. They worked out an arrangement so they could both use one of our two mules. Somehow, in those days before instant messaging and mobile devices, they each managed to have a full team when they needed it and each worked up a full crop that year.

Dad could have turned down our neighbor's request. It certainly would have been easier not to have to transport the mule back and forth between farms, but Dad cared enough about the other farmer to make the extra effort. Dad's actions remind me of what Jesus said during the Last Supper, just after the Lord had washed His disciples' feet: "just as I have loved you, you also are to love one another" (John 13:34).

Loving others means much more than just thinking nice thoughts about them or even just treating them kindly. Jesus commanded us to love as He loves, which means actively serving one another and giving of ourselves sacrificially. If we only help others when it is easy or convenient to do so, then we are putting our own interests first and staying focused on ourselves. On the other hand, when we do not have abundant resources but still intentionally give or serve, then we are stating with our actions that the needs of others are more important to us than our own. As Dr. David Jeremiah states in his book *Signs of Life*, "We declare Christ's love with our mouths, but we demonstrate it with our muscles."[1]

My brother Lloyd Junior followed in Dad's footsteps and also provided a good example of what it means to love intentionally. Of the older siblings, Lloyd Junior lived closest to Mom and Dad. During the time that I was still living at home with my parents, Lloyd and his wife, Lois, would make the two-hour trip down from Birmingham nearly every month to see Mom and Dad and help them out with smaller things around the farm. Lois would work in the kitchen with Mom, and Lloyd Junior would labor outside with Dad and us younger boys.

In addition to those regular visits, Lloyd and Lois

made a special trip down each Labor Day. Lloyd Junior would get the day off from his job at Alabama Cast Iron Pipe Company, and he and Lois would drive down to Marion on Sunday night. Around the first of September was a big time for picking cotton. Lloyd would go out with us on Monday morning and begin picking cotton as if he'd never left the farm. Even though he didn't spend as much time in the fields as we did anymore, he could still beat us younger guys. We'd finish up around four o'clock and head back to the house, where Mom and Lois

My dad, my brothers and I join Lloyd Junior's family for a group photo. I am standing in the center.

had cooked up a feast of fried chicken and homemade ice cream. We enjoyed sitting around the table, talking and laughing together. After we'd all finished, Lois would help clean up the dishes before she and Lloyd Junior headed back to Birmingham that night.

It may not sound like much, making a monthly trip and helping with farm work, but consider the situation. Lloyd and Lois were still what you would call newlyweds. They were in the midst of building a life together and didn't have a lot of time or money to spare for traveling. That said, they knew how much their visits meant to Mom and Dad, especially since most of the other siblings were not able to come as frequently. They also knew that there was still plenty of work to do on the farm and not as many hands to do it at that time. Instead of just taking care of themselves, they made the effort to take care of our family, too. They showed love by giving of themselves.

Lloyd showed godly love not only to our family but to me personally. My brother Lloyd Junior was a big baseball fan, and his favorite team was the Brooklyn Dodgers. If you cut him, he'd probably bleed Dodger blue. In 1963, between my junior and senior year of high school, Lloyd sprung for tickets for the two of us to go to a weekend series in Cincinnati, Ohio, where the Dodgers were playing the Cincinnati Reds. Lloyd asked Dad's permission to take me before anything else was decided; I was going to be gone from Thursday to Monday, which meant Dad had to do all the farm work in that time. I reckon Dad knew how much it would mean to me, because he agreed right away.

On August 9, 1963, Lloyd Junior and I went to Crosley Field to watch our Dodgers play. The Reds and the Dodgers played three games that weekend, and the Dodgers won one out of the three. I got to see Johnny Podres, Sandy Koufax, and Don Drysdale pitch that weekend. Sitting in the stands with such great players right there in front of me, I couldn't get my eyes big enough to take everything in. I can't even imagine what I must have looked like.

Since then, I've been blessed to travel all over the world, but that weekend and the fact that my brother thought enough of me to take me meant more than any other trip I've taken. My brother was not well off, but he paid for the whole trip — tickets, food, travel expenses, everything. I tried to do things later to repay him, but whatever I gave him did not even come close to what he had given me. Lloyd sacrificed so much to do something I'll never forget.

~

Among the Lord's commandments in the Old Testament is this: "You shall love your neighbor as yourself." When asked which of the commandments was most important, Jesus stated that loving one's neighbor is second only to loving God, and those two are above all else. Who is our neighbor, then, that we should so willingly give of ourselves for his good? When this question was put to our Lord by a lawyer seeking to justify himself, Jesus answered with the parable of the Good Samaritan, recounted in chapter 10 of the book of Luke:

A man was going down from Jerusalem to Jericho, and he fell among robbers, who stripped him and beat him and departed, leaving him half dead. Now by chance a priest was going down that road, and when he saw him he passed by on the other side. So likewise a Levite, when he came to the place and saw him, passed by on the other side. But a Samaritan, as he journeyed, came to where he was, and when he saw him, he had compassion. He went to him and bound up his

wounds, pouring on oil and wine. Then he set him
on his own animal and brought him to an inn
and took care of him. And the next day he took
out two denarii and gave them to the innkeeper,
saying, "Take care of him, and whatever more you
spend, I will repay you when I come back."

Now, the hearers of the parable at the time would
have expected either the priest or the Levite to stop and
aid the injured man; after all, they were both religious
leaders and supposedly moral men. Instead, it was the
Samaritan who stopped. This is especially significant
because, at the time, Jews and Samaritans had a centu-
ries-old hatred of each other. Although both groups were
descended from the nation of Israel, disagreements of
belief and religious practice had caused them to develop
bitterness and resentment towards each other. Normally,
Jews and Samaritans would have no dealings with each
other whatsoever; therefore, for a Samaritan to go out of
his way to help a Jew would have been unheard of.

It can be surmised that Jesus presented this unlikely
scenario to further emphasize the extent to which
our love and compassion for others should reach. The
Samaritan in the parable went far beyond what might be

considered common decency today, even if one doesn't take the existing animosity into account. He took care of the man's immediate needs (which is where many of us might stop), but then went the extra mile — literally! — to ensure that the man would continue to receive care. The Samaritan sacrificed his time, comfort, and money to help a stranger, and all he would have been able to tell initially by looking was that the man was a Jew in need.

In Old Testament law, there are many commandments to the Israelites concerning how each man should treat his neighbor. The context of those commandments seems to imply that a neighbor is someone of the same tribe or nation, and the lawyer who asked Jesus to define the term certainly seemed to be angling for such a delineation so that his responsibility to his fellow man would be within comfortable boundaries. Rather than basing the definition of "neighbor" on sameness or even physical proximity, Jesus demonstrated through His story that a neighbor is anyone is need.

Today, in our increasingly connected global community, our neighbors could be a local family in which one of the parents has recently been laid off, or elderly residents of another state that has experienced a natural disaster, or children in a country thousands of miles away who have never eaten a decent meal. In earlier times, it would have been difficult if not impossible to access certain parts of the world, but now, with developing technology and improved means of transportation, it is possible to reach every corner of the world with the lovingkindness of Jesus Christ.

In His follow-up question to the lawyer, Jesus turned the focus of the discussion from who our neighbors are to what kind of neighbors we should be: "Which of these three, do you think, proved to be a neighbor to the man who fell among the robbers?"

The lawyer, unable to absolve himself of responsibility with a counterargument, answered, "The one who showed him mercy."

Jesus' final statement was a commandment not only to the lawyer and others who were listening at the time, but to all of us: "You go, and do likewise."

Following this commandment is not always easy. Truly loving one's neighbor often requires self-sacrifice of some kind, whether that be of money, time, or physical energy. Sometimes, a situation may even require an emotional sacrifice. Showing love to a person who responds with warmth and gratitude is rewarding for both parties in the moment; however, to love someone when that person can't — or won't — return the favor takes a truly Spirit-fueled attitude. This lesson was demonstrated to me firsthand by my mother.

When I was a boy of eight or nine, my parents drove us to Selma to pick up some supplies for the farm. As we walked by a drugstore, I noticed it had an ice cream counter. I ran inside, climbed up on the stool, and asked the man behind the counter for an ice cream cone. He just stood there looking at me; a moment later, my mother strode in, snatched me up, and pulled me out of there. I didn't understand why I couldn't get an ice cream cone; as a child, I wouldn't have noticed the sign saying "Whites Only." On the drive home, my mother told me I shouldn't do that anymore, but I don't know that she ever told me the reason why.

As we grew up, our folks taught us what to do if we found ourselves in certain situations, but they didn't teach us to be hateful. My parents loved the Lord and taught us to love, even when it was difficult to do so. The man in the drugstore was a product of his time, and he chose not to challenge the status quo that day by allowing something society would frown upon. My mother probably did more to better the storekeeper's opinion of African-Americans by graciously leaving than she would have by challenging his attitude. In the words of Dr. Martin Luther King, Jr., "Darkness cannot drive out darkness; only light can do that. Hate cannot drive out hate; only love can do that."[2]

It is important to remember that God's command to love others as yourself is not dependent on that love being returned. In fact, Jesus directly countered the idea that love must be two-sided when He commanded His listeners to "love your enemies and pray for those who persecute you, so that you may be sons of your Father who is in heaven" (Matthew 5:44-45).

Although that goes counter to our human understanding of justice, it is completely aligned with the example of our Lord's unconditional love. Despite being mocked, beaten, and despised, Jesus still offered love and forgiveness to those responsible for His crucifixion. Despite being disparaged, devalued, and denied, God still offers love and forgiveness to a fallen world today.

"God's love is not some vaporous feeling that ebbs and flows with unpredictable undercurrents and uncertain tides. God's love is a divine attribute that is as strong as steel, as solid as granite, and as deliberate as a marching army. [...] Now, since Jesus loves us with such deliberate, purposeful love, shouldn't we love with that same kind of love? In terms of loving others with Jesus' love, His example means discovering and meeting people's needs. In terms of loving God, Jesus' example means obeying Him."[3] When we pattern our lives after Christ's example, we are more in tune with His Spirit; thus, we grow closer to God Himself by loving His people.

~

1. What did Lloyd Harper and his neighbor each gain by sharing a mule?

_____

_____

_____

_____

2. What did Lloyd Junior sacrifice in order to demonstrate his love for his parents and brother? What effects did his sacrifice have on his family at the time and long-term?

_____

_____

_____

_____

3. In the parable of the Good Samaritan, why do you think the priest and the Levite did not stop to offer aid? Why do you think the Samaritan did?

_____

_____

_____

_____

4. Have you ever been in a situation in which it was difficult to love someone? How did you overcome those difficulties?

_____

_____

_____

_____

5. Who are some "neighbors" in your life, and how can you love them better?

_____

_____

_____

_____

CHAPTER SEVEN

A THANKFUL HEART

The love that God asks us to extend to others unconditionally is but a miniscule fraction of the love He shows us. Every good thing that we enjoy in this life — whether it be something awe-inspiring such as miraculous healing from a disease or something as simple as knowing there is oxygen for our next breath — is a palpable sign of God's love for us. The fact that God has given with such love should prompt us to respond in gratitude and demonstrate our joy for His pleasure. That means, in part, taking time each day to thank God for all His many graces; it also means not taking the privileges He has given us by means of birth or situation for granted.

During the 1950s and 1960s, African-American citizens in Alabama were given special voting tests. They had to answer all of the questions correctly in order to become registered voters, which effectively prevented most from being able to vote. Caucasians were not given these tests because it was assumed they were intelligent enough to participate in an election.

When I was a young man in high school, my mom and dad tried many times to earn their right to vote. They would go to the polling area to take a written test of about ten questions, which included things like "Who was the twenty-fifth President of the United States?" and "Who was the Governor of Alabama in 1942?"

They of course would not be able to answer all the questions. When my parents returned from the polling station, I would look up information on all the questions they could remember and help them learn the right answers; however, each time they went back to take the test, the questions had been changed, and they would fail the test again. Although my parents were folks who showed little emotion, I could see their disappointment each time they could not pass the tests. Each failed attempt was a tremendous blow to their pride.

My parents had a general tendency not to accept the status quo. It was that tendency that led to them being landowners in a time when most African-Americans were sharecroppers. In all aspects of life, my parents never gave up fighting for what they believed was right, and this situation was no exception. In keeping with the spirit of our country's founders, when they felt pushed down by unfair limitations, they pushed back with quiet determination.

My parents were also very patriotic. They loved and honored the flag of the United States and encouraged their children to do so also. Of the six able young men, five of us — Richard, Lloyd Junior, Eddie, Jefferson Davis and I — proudly served in the U.S. military. Mom and Dad believed that being a citizen of the United States entailed not only unalienable rights but also indisputable duties, of which voting responsibly was one.

Eventually, the federal government forced the rules to be changed so that African-Americans were no longer required to take tests to qualify to vote. Dad and Mom were so excited to get a chance to vote in the 1960 presidential election, with John F. Kennedy running against Richard Milhous Nixon. They watched all the debates in order to make an informed decision. I thought they were going to vote for Kennedy and was surprised to hear that they voted for Nixon. I asked them why they had chosen Nixon, and they said they had heard the television commentators express concerns about Kennedy's religious beliefs.

That in itself was a valuable lesson; when my parents

were finally enabled to vote, they made a commitment to always use that privilege to vote for the one they believed would honor God. Their gratitude fueled their desire to glorify God through their choices. The 1960 election was the only presidential election my dad got a chance to vote in before his death, but he made it count in the only way that matters.

In modern American culture, a large number of those who are able to vote do not exercise this right, and many of those who do vote do so without having devoted much thought or prayer to their choice of candidates. It is unlikely that any election (other than that of an extraordinarily small town) would be decided by one vote, so, in that, it is possible for naysayers to argue that one's vote doesn't really matter; however, I wholeheartedly disagree with this viewpoint. Perhaps yours will not be the deciding vote in an election that will change the course of our country's history, but the fact that you are free to endorse a man or woman whom you believe to be someone who would lead in a godly manner is not a privilege to be taken lightly. Charles Colson, founder of BreakPoint Ministries, observed that "God has placed us in our cities and neighborhoods to reflect his character and to restore his righteous dominion in the midst of a fallen world. We begin with our personal lives and habits, move out from there to our families and schools and then into our communities — and from there into our society as a whole."[1]

~

In trying circumstances, we can either focus on our frustrations or thank God for His mercies within the storm. The Bible gives examples of both attitudes so that we can learn from both.

Probably the most notorious case of ingratitude in Scripture is that of the Israelites after they had been rescued from slavery in Egypt. God had demonstrated His power and His care for the nation of Israel by inflicting plagues on the unrelenting Egyptians but sparing His people. When the worst plague, the death of the firstborns, fell upon the Egyptians, the Lord made it very clear that He was sparing the Israelites for His purpose. He brought them out of Egypt and through the midst of the Red Sea on dry ground, and at that time the people of Israel did praise the Lord for His majesty and salvation. They even expressed their faith that God would continue His mercies to their people, saying,

"You will bring them in and plant them on your own mountain, the place, O Lord, which you have made for your abode, the sanctuary, O Lord, which your hands have established. The Lord will reign forever and ever" (Exodus 15:17-18).

The Israelites' gratitude was short-lived, however; just three days after their time of worship, the Israelites lost faith that God would provide for them. They had not yet found water, but instead of submitting their request to God, they began to grumble. God demonstrated the depth of His mercy in His response, immediately meeting their need rather than condemning their attitude. Not only did He give them clean, sweet water to drink in that moment, but He also brought them to a place of refreshment that could more than satisfy their thirst.

Rather than learning from the experience, the Israelites continued to undervalue their deliverance. A few weeks later, after the food they had brought with them had been exhausted, the Israelites began to grumble again. This time, they expressed not only a lack of faith in what God *would* do but a lack of appreciation in what God *had* done: "And the whole congregation of the people of Israel grumbled against Moses and Aaron in the wilderness, and the people of Israel said to them,

'Would that we had died by the hand of the Lord in the land of Egypt, when we sat by the meat pots and ate bread to the full, for you have brought us out into this wilderness to kill this whole assembly with hunger'" (Exodus 16:3).

Rather than trusting that the God who had only a short time before proven His awesome power by rescuing them through miraculous means could bring them through their present difficulty to a place of blessing, the Israelites cried out for the supposed safety of the familiar, no matter how horrible it might be. As Matthew Henry noted in his commentary, "They pronounce it better to have fallen in the destruction of God's enemies than to bear the fatherly discipline of his children! We cannot suppose that they had any great plenty in Egypt, how largely soever they now talk of the flesh-pots; nor could they fear dying for want in the wilderness, while they had their flocks and herds with them. But discontent magnifies what is past, and vilifies what is present, without regard to truth or reason."[2]

Proving His infinite mercy, God once again met their need, sending manna and quails in miraculous quantities. Again and again, this pattern was repeated during the Israelites' sojourn to the Promised Land

— the Israelites allowed what they could see and feel to taint what they knew about God, but God remained faithful in His promise to them.

It is easy to look at the example of the Israelites and vilify them for their weakness, but how often do we do the same? How many of us, with food in the pantry and clothes in the closet, will bemoan some aspect of our lives that is not going according to plan? When it comes to the posture of the heart, it is amazing how similar some of us are to the ungrateful children of Israel. Thankfully, the Lord offers the same grace and mercy to us in our times of despair and distrust. "When we begin to fret and be uneasy, we ought to consider that God hears all our murmurings, though silent, and only the murmurings of the heart. Princes, parents, masters, do not hear all the murmurs of their inferiors against them [...]; but God hears, and yet bears."[3]

Contrast the attitude of the children of Israel with that of Daniel. When the kingdom of Judah was in decline, the Babylonians besieged Jerusalem. They took Daniel and many other young men captive, carrying them back to Babylon to serve in the king's palace. Their position was privileged but tenuous because it depended on the whim of the king; stories throughout the Book of

Daniel show that the king might sentence any number of his servants to death for any reason of his choosing. As far as we can tell from Scripture, Daniel and the others never returned to their homes or families in Judah. Their beliefs were tested, their heritage suppressed, and yet Daniel found opportunities to thank God in the midst of it all.

One such opportunity came when King Nebuchadnezzar was troubled by strange dreams. The king set an impossible task before his wise men and magicians — to interpret his dreams without being told their contents. Of course, the sorcerers and their pagan gods could not meet the king's request, and the king responded in wrath, commanding that all the wise men in Babylon — including Daniel — be put to death. Daniel, trusting in God to give him wisdom, requested an audience with the king. After a time of prayer, God did indeed reveal the mystery of the king's dream, and Daniel responded with unmitigated praise: "Blessed be the name of God forever and ever, to whom belong wisdom and might. [...] To you, O God of my fathers, I give thanks and praise, for you have given me wisdom and might, and have now made known to me what we asked of you" (Daniel 2:20, 23).

The king did promote Daniel for his service and was, for the moment, appreciative of Daniel and his God. However, immediately after the account of Nebuchadnezzar giving gifts and high honors to Daniel and his friends is the account of the king erecting a golden idol for all to worship, under penalty of death. Although the climate of the court was ever-changing, Daniel's faith did not waver. His gratefulness to God was not dependent on the king's favor but on who God is.

~

Throughout my youth, my parents demonstrated the same trust in and gratitude to God that Daniel did. They always found something to be grateful for, even if it was just waking up in the morning to live and serve another day. I learned from them early on that thankfulness is not based on circumstances, but the lesson was particularly reinforced during my time in the military.

At the time I was drafted, I did not want to go into the Army. I wasn't political at the time and didn't have any fight with the Viet Cong. I even considered going to Canada to avoid the draft, but, praise God, I decided to honor the call to military service. In September of 1966,

I went to Fort Carson, Colorado, to train as an infan-
tryman for eight months. This included eight weeks
of basic training and eight weeks of advanced infantry
training.

I was assigned to Company C, along with five
hundred other young men. Once I began training in
earnest, my upbringing started to kick in. I thought of
my dad, who could outwork anyone, and decided that
whatever this new situation threw at me, I would give
it my best effort. I had no idea what I was capable of or
if my best effort would be good enough in the Army.
That was the first time I had competed with Caucasians,
having been raised in a segregated community and
having attended an African-American high school.

During basic training, we went through a series of
written and oral examinations to determine our aptitude
as soldiers. We were tested on our physical prowess, our
knowledge of standard operational procedures such
as salutes and maneuvers, and our ability to carry out
orders. We also practiced marksmanship, in which I
excelled. Towards the end of our training, those of us
who were doing especially well went through a practical
examination under the observation of several of our
superiors.

Awards were given out during our graduation from basic training. I did not expect to receive any accolades; I knew I had done my best, but there were many diligent young men in my unit. Suddenly, I heard my name being called. Hands shaking, I stepped up to the front and was shocked to hear that not only was I being honored for my accomplishments, but that I was the trainee with the best overall performance in Company C. I don't know if anyone else at the ceremony was surprised to hear that I was the top trainee, but I certainly was.

That single recognition served as a catalyst for me to pursue with confidence other achievements throughout my life thus far. God not only blessed me with the mental and physical abilities to succeed, but He also raised me up to a level of recognition that I could never have dreamed of. As it says in Proverbs 18:16, the gifts that God gives a man are what open the doors for that man to succeed. Almost fifty years later, I still display the Army trophy proudly on my desk in my office because it is a trophy of God's grace to me.

God continued to extend grace throughout my military career as well. I was not sent to fight in Vietnam as I had feared; instead, I served in Korea for fourteen months. I arrived in Korea in April of 1967 and was initially assigned to the supply area of my battalion. I was promoted to the rank of Sergeant E-5 in October 1967, only thirteen months after entering active duty. That early promotion is another testimony to God's gracious gifting. I returned to the United States in June of 1968 and was given an honorable discharge, which was customary at that time for any soldier who had less than ninety days of active duty left at the time of his return. As grateful as I was for all of God's blessings during my time in the military, I was even more grateful to be going home.

The many blessings that God gave to me during my time in the military showed me how closely related a trusting heart and a thankful spirit are. If we trust that God will provide and is providing what we need in every circumstance, then we have the opportunity to thank Him constantly, not only for what He has given but also for what we know He will give. A saying that I have often used over the years is, "If God did that for me there, He could do that for me here."

Often, our appreciation for a gift is rooted in our appreciation of the giver. A flower, which is beautiful on its own, becomes immeasurably more precious when it is given by a husband to his wife, because she associates the flower with his love. Likewise, we can look at wonders such as a beautiful sunrise or a towering poplar tree and see expressions of the Father's great love for us. Dr. David Jeremiah points out, "We're not just rich because of God's blessings; we're rich because of God Himself. He is our treasure and our exceeding great reward."[4] By thanking God for what He has given, we are also thanking Him for who He is.

How, then, can we possibly begin to show our thanks to God for His innumerable blessings and infinite goodness? According to Colossians 3:15-17, our thankfulness to God should be a constant posture of the heart that spills over as love to His people: "And let the peace of Christ rule in your hearts, to which indeed you were called in one body. And be thankful. Let the word of Christ dwell in you richly, teaching and admonishing one another in all wisdom, singing psalms and hymns and spiritual songs, with thankfulness in your hearts to God. And whatever you do, in word or deed, do everything in the name of the Lord Jesus, giving thanks to God the Father through him."

Christians are called to be thankful for the same reason that we are called to be loving and joyful and patient and gracious — that the name of Jesus may be revered throughout the earth, that all peoples may know Him and glorify Him.

~

1. Part of having an attitude of gratitude is noticing the little blessings that God dispenses moment by moment. What are three things from today for which you can be thankful?

_____

_____

_____

_____

2. How did Lloyd and Walter Mae Harper demonstrate their thankfulness for finally having the freedom to vote? How can you demonstrate your thankfulness for one of the things named above?

_____

_____

_____

_____

3. Why do you think the Israelites struggled to see God's provision? What can you do to help another believer who is stuck in a similar pattern of grumbling?

_____

_____

_____

_____

4. What enabled Daniel to praise God when his life was at stake?

_____

_____

_____

_____

5. How does having a thankful attitude impact other aspects of life? How can it impact others?

_____

_____

_____

_____

CHAPTER EIGHT

ALL FOR THE GLORY OF GOD

As I mentioned in the previous chapter, a large part of demonstrating one's thankfulness is utilizing the gift with the giver in mind. Not only does this help us to continue in a spirit of gratitude long after we have received the gift, but it also allows us to openly honor and actively love the giver, which creates a circle of blessing.

If we, God's creation, derive joy from seeing our gifts well loved by the recipients, how much more so does God, who has given us everything, derive joy from the glory attributed to Him by His children! God has provided each of us with specific gifts, and it is His providential will to direct us to the place that He has designed for us to utilize our gifts for His glory. When we are playing and having fun, God wants us to rejoice in Him. When He allows us to succeed in our work, God wants us to praise Him for His provision.

God's provision may not always come by the easiest or most pleasant path, but if we are faithful to trust

Him, God will always lead us to the place that will bring Himself the most glory and do us the most good. Probably the best example of this in Scripture is the account of Joseph's life in Genesis 37 and 39-47. Joseph began life as the favored son of Jacob, who had already been promised great prosperity by God; however, his life took an unexpected turn when he was sold into slavery by his brothers. This apparent setback took Joseph to Egypt, where he then prospered anew as a trusted servant in the house of Potiphar, who was captain of Pharaoh's guard.

The Bible makes it clear that the success Joseph achieved while serving in Potiphar's house was made possible through God's blessing and Joseph's desire to use his present position to glorify God. Joseph's love for God prevented him from violating God's law with Potiphar's wife; and although Joseph's rejection of her ultimately landed him in prison, God was still working in Joseph's life. Once again, Joseph remained devoted to the Lord despite his circumstances, and once again God blessed Joseph's faithfulness by elevating him to a privileged position. Genesis 39:23 says, "The warden paid no attention to anything under Joseph's care, because the Lord was with Joseph and gave him success in whatever he did."

When Joseph was a young man still in his father's

house, God gave him the gift of dream interpretation. While in prison, God gave Joseph the opportunity to use his gift, and Joseph in turn gave God the credit for his abilities. By successfully interpreting the royal cupbearer's dream, Joseph eventually gained audience with Pharaoh himself, who also had troublesome dreams. God used Joseph to deliver a warning through his interpretation, so that Egypt would be prepared for the coming famine. Joseph again took no credit for himself, but gave all glory to God; and, miraculously, the pagan Pharaoh recognized God's power and rewarded His servant with a position that was second-in-command in all the land.

At every junction of Joseph's life, the Bible makes it clear that God was shaping events for Joseph's benefit; as Joseph's story unfolds, we also see the glory gained by God through the faithfulness of his servant. God chose to save the Egyptian people and people from the surrounding lands from starvation by sending a warning through a dream, but things could not have come to pass in that way if Joseph had not devoted his life to God's glory.

~

Working for the glory of God means giving God

your best. Whatever resources we have — time, abilities, connections — are ours because God has given them to us for our good and the good of His kingdom. He hasn't called us to live unproductive, self-fulfilling lives; on the contrary, every moment of our brief time on earth should be seen as a precious opportunity to pursue excellence in Christ.

Ephesians 2:10 says, "For we are his workmanship, created in Christ Jesus for good works, which God prepared beforehand, that we should walk in them." The word that is translated as workmanship is the Greek *poiema*, the root of the English word "poem"; thus, we could say that each of us is God's poem, that He is the great Author writing the verses of our lives. I responded to this truth by writing a poem of my own:

> *God saved this son of a farmer*
> *And directed him to a life as a teacher,*
> *A teacher who began by stuttering,*
> *Quite unsure and with little self-esteem.*
> *But God, who created and designed self-confidence,*
> *Provided a way for him to gain some*
> *Then to share some*
> *And then to teach some.*

The "good work" God prepared for my dad was farming. It may not have been exciting or glamorous, but Dad took his calling seriously and served God to the utmost through the fruits of his labor.

In the 1930s, the government began regulating how many acres a farmer could use for planting certain cash crops in order to prevent the market from being flooded and prices being driven down. Dad was limited to planting ten acres of cotton (although if he had had his choice he would have planted fifty), but he decided to do the most he could within that limitation.

Most farmers thought they were doing great if they were able to produce one bale of cotton per acre, which amounted to about five hundred pounds of pure cotton after the seeds were extracted at the cotton gin. Dad averaged about a bale and a half per acre. He was able to maximize his revenue while still staying within the boundaries that were set for him.

By observing how Dad excelled despite his limitations, I learned at a young age the benefits of making the most out of what you have been given. Later, when I entered the business world, I analyzed Dad's approach to cotton growing and adapted it to apply to any position of management. The basic idea of "Top Turn" is to yield the maximum output with minimal resources. Rather than focusing on what can't be done because of some obstacle or limitation, look for ways to work around it or excel within it.

Later, when I was working at Goodyear, I saw this principle put into practice by Stan Mihelick and Jerry Butcher, two innovative leaders of The Goodyear Tire & Rubber Company's manufacturing operations. They would challenge various tire plants to identify the bottleneck area in their production process, whatever step was taking the most time and slowing down production. They found that production was most often slowing down in the curing cycle, where pressure and heat are applied in a mold to give the tire its final shape. Stan and Jerry put chemical and engineering experts in place at the various manufacturing plants to find a way to reduce curing time while still producing a world-class tire. Whenever curing time could be reduced by even one second, it resulted in more tires being produced each day and increased the possibility of generating more revenue.

Stan and Jerry, to increase and improve production, also used an approach called the Perfection Strategy. When they would go into a plant, even one that was not very efficient, they would look for one aspect of the plant's operations that was functioning especially well. It could be a step in the manufacturing process, an effective management technique, or some other factor. After identifying this "pocket of perfection," Stan and Jerry would use its success as a gauge for the potential success of the plant as a whole. Their goal was to get every part of the plant — workers, machinery, methods, materials, etc. — up to the standard of the plant's best practices.

The idea of the Perfection Strategy is that it is necessary to define the goals we are working towards so that we have motivation to move forward; without goals, we are likely to become lazy and complacent. Rather than settling for "good enough," we should be striving for the best! Throughout the Bible there is evidence that God encourages overachievers; for example, 2 Timothy 2:15 directs believers to "do your best to present yourself to God as one approved, a worker who has no need to be ashamed, rightly handling the word of truth."

Think of the example we have before us in the Lord Himself. He did not cut corners when He was crafting the universe. Instead, He created something beautiful and majestic that would not only demonstrate His magnitude but also bring us joy. He made us, His

people, with such intricately interconnected systems
that modern medicine still does not grasp every facet
of the body's functions. But even in biblical times, when
comprehension of the complexities of the human body
was limited, the psalmist knew that he was a master-
piece: "I praise you, for I am fearfully and wonderfully
made. Wonderful are your works; my soul knows it very
well" (Psalm 139:14).

~

For some, the difficulty is not identifying a goal but
obtaining it. Effecting change, whether in a business or
in the life of an individual, involves identifying existing
hindrances through Top Turn analysis and employing the
Perfection Strategy to push towards levels of excellence
that have never been reached before. When teaching this
concept, I often use a mathematical equation to show
how the various factors work together:

$$PC \ (planned \ change) = D + M + TP > C$$

The D stands for dissatisfaction with the status quo.
You may have heard it said that the first step to recovery

is admitting you have a problem; without this realization that something about the current state of things is bad or at least could be better, there is no motivation to change. On the other hand, with the right perspective, dissatisfaction actually can be a good thing. It is what prompts a person or organization to act.

The M stands for a model of your desired future state. This hearkens back to the Perfection Strategy, wherein a person or organization identifies the ideal outcome to work towards. In imagining the desired future state, it is helpful to use as much detail as possible. Having a specific goal enables you to know when you've reached it. For example, a businessman may desire for his company to manufacture more goods, but setting a goal to increase production by 30 percent allows him to know when he and his company have achieved success in this manner. The same is true for an individual. If your goal is to lose weight, be specific about how many pounds you want to lose and how much you want to weigh in the end.

Once you have been motivated to act and have established a desired outcome, the next step is to develop a transition plan (TP) to reach your goal. The transition plan is like a map to a destination. It's not enough to know where you want to go — you have to know how to get there, too. If you want to lose twenty pounds, make a plan to get up each day at 5:00 a.m. and spend forty-five minutes on the treadmill. If you aim to increase sales for your company by 10 percent, talk to other successful salespeople and figure out a system that will enable you to reach that goal.

The "greater than" symbol (>) means that the various factors that lead to planned change must be considered by the individual as more important than the cost of doing nothing (C). To continue with an earlier example, the cost of losing weight may be time out of a busy schedule or money for a gym membership, but in order for change to happen, that cost must be considered less than the potential cost of not losing weight — sleep apnea, diabetes, or heart disease. The benefits of the planned change — feeling better, looking better, and having more energy — would also outweigh cost in this model. In short, this model is true when a person is willing to do whatever it takes to reach the end, because the end is worth it.

~

Looking back at Dad's life, it is clear that he did not

just work to get by. At no time was Dad's dedication more evident than in the final weeks of his life. The year I graduated from high school, 1964, was the year my dad died. His kidneys started to fail that August, and he was admitted to the Marion hospital for treatment. He was sick enough to die right then, but I think he bargained with the Lord. Since we had no medical insurance, Dad may have been thinking about how the hospital bill would be paid. I think he told the Lord that he didn't want to leave before the crop was harvested.

I had been awarded a scholarship to attend Stillman College in Tuscaloosa that fall. I was dead set on going straight to college and didn't know how that crop was going to get picked. I soon got my answer. My sister Eleanor called me one night and said, "You're gonna have to stay there and get that crop out of the field."

I asked her, "Why me?"

She replied, "Because you're the only one of us kids who's still there on the farm."

I couldn't argue with her reasoning and reluctantly agreed to take care of the harvest; once I got going with it, though, the process proved to be very rewarding.

At seventeen years of age, I became the man of the house and the manager of the farm. I was responsible for hiring field workers, negotiating their wages, providing transportation to those who needed it, challenging those who slacked off or fell behind, and dealing with any issues that arose. I was leading people who were a lot older than me, but I earned their respect by treating them fairly and doing my job well. That experience was probably the greatest management training I've ever had, and it really set me up for later successes. The best part was coming back to the house in the evenings and seeing the satisfaction in my mom's eyes, knowing that she was proud of how I was handling everything.

On October 22, we finished picking all the cotton. I went to the hospital that morning to pick up Mom and take her home to get some rest. While I was there at the hospital, I had the pleasure of telling Dad that his last cotton crop had been harvested and seeing a calmness come over his face. I didn't know it at the time, but that was the news he had been waiting for.

My brother Richard had just been honorably discharged from the service, and I went to pick him up from the bus station in Selma later that day. The two of us went back to the hospital so that Richard could see Dad, but when we arrived, we were met in the hallway by Lee Benson, who told us Dad had already passed away.

I have no doubt that Dad had died happy, knowing that his work was complete.

The harvest of 1964 represented the culmination of Dad's life's labors. Although I was the one who was there in body to oversee every task, it was for my dad's sake and to his credit that we brought in an excellent crop of cotton that year. Over the years, Dad had laid the foundation for the farm to succeed, planting not only the literal seeds in the ground but also seeds of knowledge and wisdom in me. The work I did during the harvest that year was not to earn praise for myself but to please my dad and preserve his legacy.

That experience of working so that Dad could get the credit has helped me to better understand how our lives are meant to glorify the name of God. Each of us has received a call to serve in some capacity. Through our service, we will likely gain spiritual maturity and wisdom and may receive personal commendation and rewards for our work; however, the One for whom we are laboring is the One who rightfully deserves the praise. Any opportunity we have in which we can excel has been given to us by God; and everything we do, even the most mundane task, affords an opportunity to glorify God with the fruits of our labor. If God is getting credit for the fruits of our lives, shouldn't we be offering Him the best?

Glorifying God isn't an add-on or an afterthought — it is the entire purpose of our existence. 1 Corinthians 10:31 says, "So, whether you eat or drink, or whatever you do, do all to the glory of God." It may at first seem odd to our sensibilities that we are to spend our lifetime working so that someone else can have the credit, but it becomes entirely comprehensible when we remember who that Someone is. God is the only being in the universe who is absolutely worthy of all the glory we can possibly ascribe to Him (and more). We cannot make God any more excellent or awesome than he already is; glorifying God does not add to Him. Rather, "God created us for this: to live our lives in a way that makes him look more like the greatness and the beauty and the infinite worth that He really is."[1]

The wonderful thing about glorifying God is that, true to His character, He uses our act of exalting Him to enrich our own lives and the lives of those around us. A life that is focused on Christ is a life that is truly satisfying. For ourselves, we have the assurance "that the God of our Lord Jesus Christ, the Father of glory, may give you the Spirit of wisdom and of revelation in the knowledge of him, having the eyes of your hearts enlightened, that you may know what is the hope to which he has called you, what are the riches of his glorious inheritance in the saints, and what is the immeasurable greatness of his power toward us who believe, according to the working of his great might" (Ephesians 1:17-19).

For others, our glorification of God can be a window through which to see His marvelous attributes. Matthew 5:16 tells us to "let your light shine before others, so that they may see your good works and give glory to your Father who is in heaven." If each of us responds to this verse with obedience, it may produce a ripple effect of renewed devotion within the Church body; or, even better, it may bring some who are walking in darkness to a saving knowledge of Jesus Christ. That is a goal truly worth working towards.

~

1. *How was God glorified through Joseph's life?*

_____

_____

_____

_____

2. *How can God be glorified through work that is not specifically related to the Church or missions? What action can you take to glorify God through your work this week? How about long-term?*

_____

_____

_____

_____

3. *Who is credited with the success of the 1964 harvest and why?*

_____

_____

_____

_____

4. *How do you think simple actions like eating and drinking can bring glory to God?*

_____

_____

_____

_____

5. How does the act of glorifying God affect the world around us?

_____

_____

_____

_____

CHAPTER NINE

MAKING HIS WILL YOUR WILL

Knowing the will of God is both one of the easiest and hardest aspects of the Christian life. On the one hand, we know unquestionably that we are all called to love God and glorify Him in all we do. We also know that we are to make disciples (Matthew 28:19), to imitate Christ (Ephesians 5:1), and to give to the poor and needy (Matthew 5:42); these are fundamental practices of the faith that apply to all believers at all times, which the Bible makes clear. But what about when it comes to knowing whether or not God would have you take that new job or buy that new house? How do we know when God wants us to act and when He wants us to remain where we are? Sometimes living in the will of God means stepping towards an open door, and sometimes it means stepping back from an opportunity. I have been called to do both at different times in my life, but the way in which I have discerned God's direction has always been the same.

As you learned in the previous chapter, my dad died in October 1964 after my senior year of high school. Because it was already well into Stillman College's fall term, I decided to wait to start there until the following year. That next summer, I went to stay with my sister Ruth and her husband, Thompson, in Chicago. To save up money for tuition, I took a job working as a research lab operator at Michael Reese Hospital for $1.25 an hour ($37.50 per week after taxes). It was my responsibility to clean up the lab after experiments and to take care of the animals (mostly rabbits) that were used as test subjects. I went to the lab to feed them seven days a week. Every day after work, I'd go to the park to play baseball with some other young men.

One day, I noticed a man watching as we threw the ball around. After we had finished our game, he came up to me and asked for my name and address. I was a little suspicious of him at first, because Thompson (who was a police officer) had warned me against swindlers; however, the man identified himself as a baseball scout. I gave him my sister's address and, a few days later, received an invitation to come and try out for the Chicago White Sox.

On the day of the tryouts, I took the "L" train and

the bus out to old Comiskey Park. Ruth had bought me a brand-new glove and cleats for the occasion. There were young men of every age out there that day, from teenagers like me to twenty-somethings who were trying to break into the game. I went up to the registration table and told the men there my name; they gave me a number to wear on my back and said they would call that number when it was my turn.

There were a lot of good players there that day, and each young man was allowed to play three innings in his desired position. I was there to try out as a pitcher. When they called my number, I stepped up to the mound confidently. In my three innings, I only had to face nine batters, because not one of them got on base. I thought for sure I was on my way to a big signing bonus and the National Baseball Hall of Fame.

As it turned out, the White Sox didn't sign me on the spot. I did get a few calls later from the scouts, asking to see me two or three more times, but my brother-in-law was concerned that they might just be stringing me along. I didn't end up pursuing it, and the scouts didn't press me to come back.

Had I pursued it, who knows what might have happened? I certainly wouldn't be where I am today, doing the work I am doing; however, I don't say that with regret. If God had wanted me on the path to fame and fortune as a major league baseball player, He would have made it clear somehow. As Henry Blackaby writes in his Bible study *Experiencing God*, "Circumstances cannot always be a clear direction for God's leadership. [...] In seeking God's direction, check to see that prayer, Scripture, counsel, and circumstances agree in the direction you sense God is leading you."[1]

Psalm 37:23 says that God orders our steps if we delight in Him, and I truly believe that. Sure, at eighteen years of age, I was excited by the prospect of leaving my little hometown for the big city and seeing my name in lights, but that was not God's plan — at least, not the way I envisioned it. God did have a big plan for me that included leaving Marion, Alabama, and gaining notoriety in my field, but the path He laid out for me allowed me to draw closer to Him through every advancement and ultimately glorify Him more than myself through my success.

I stayed with Ruth from November of 1964 until I was drafted into the Army in September of 1966. During that time, I took classes as a part-time student at a local junior college. After my honorable discharge in 1968, I returned to Chicago to look for a job.

I joined Goodyear in June of 1968 as a production worker in the North Chicago hose plant. I received a bachelor of science degree in business management from Jacksonville State University in 1977 and in 1979 was promoted to a managerial position for the plant in Fayetteville, North Carolina. God continued to bless my career through several more moves up the ladder, and in 1989, I was named manager of manufacturing and support training at Goodyear's headquarters in Akron, Ohio.

My career turned towards human resources in 1996, when I became director of human resources for the North American Tire Strategic Business Unit. From there, I was promoted to vice president of human resources planning and development and, in 1998, became an elected officer and vice president of global human resource services.

When Goodyear made the decision to outsource its human resources department, I was at the forefront to ensure that the necessary transitions were made as smoothly as possible. Although most members of the department were able to stay employed after the changeover, there were many who expressed concerns at the outset. The Lord made it such that I was able to relate to their concerns in a very substantive way.

Among the many changes made during the outsourcing process was the elimination of my position as vice president of global human resource services. I remember feeling very unsettled when I saw that my job would be going away — but God had a new job for me. I became vice president of human resources for Goodyear's new North America Shared Services on December 1, 2003.

The experience definitely grew my faith in God's provision. When a company is trying to cut costs and maintain economic stability, older employees in high-paying positions are often the first to get pushed out; however, the Lord protected me through the process and blessed the good work I had done. Experiencing that uncertainty also allowed me to offer comfort to others from a position of understanding. When employees would come into my office and tell me they were worried, I would say, "Tell me about it. I've changed jobs, too."

While God was growing my career, he was also increasing my ministry. In 1997, a friend of mine told me that he had submitted my name as a candidate for the board of trustees for Malone College in Canton, Ohio (renamed Malone University in 2007). I was honored by

The Goodyear Tire & Rubber Company was recognized for a successful HR outsourcing process that was led by senior vice president of human resources, Kathy Geier, and myself, as vice president of human resources. We were honored to be featured on the cover of HRO Today *magazine in July 2004.*

his action, but I thought that my previous commitments to work, church, and my family were already almost more than I could handle; I certainly could not take on another responsibility. I agreed to meet with Malone President Dr. Ron Johnson and arrived at our breakfast appointment with every intention of telling him that I would not accept the board position.

As we got to talking, Dr. Johnson spoke of his passion for Malone's mission — to provide young men and women with a biblically sound education — and his vision for its future. His words were moving, and I found myself sharing his enthusiasm. Before we parted ways that morning, I had accepted God's call to serve on the board.

My business experience was a great asset to the board, and I had the opportunity to serve on several committees. I was even able to share my knowledge with Malone students as an executive-in-residence for three years. By 2004, God had paved the way for me to become the chairman of the board. He knew when He guided me into the business world that I would eventually use the skills He had given me to guide young people in His name. God's plan is always right and always good.

You may wonder how I knew that each career move

was the right decision at the time. To answer that, I turn again to Psalm 37:23. God has ordered every step of my walk with Him, and He has always made it clear what path He wanted me to take. Sometimes His leading comes through a sign in His word, and other times it comes through advice from a trusted friend. No matter what means God uses to speak to me, He has always been faithful to guide me at every crossroads.

The true key to knowing God's will is to stay in tune with His Spirit so that we recognize His voice when He tells us to move. If we are in a constant state of communion with God, then we will notice the divine appointments He sets up for us, the intentional detours He takes us on, the momentary nudges and insights He gives to guide our every step. Each day is full of divine opportunities that have the potential to greatly affect our lives or the lives of those around us, but many of us miss these opportunities because of distraction, hesitation, opposition, or fear. If we look beyond the chaos and confusion that surrounds us, we will see the beautiful order that God is maintaining. "Our heavenly Father wants to use the events we encounter each day as tools to shape and sculpt us in the image of Christ. He wants to deepen our faith, develop within us the quality of perseverance, and us watertight containers of His love, joy, peace, patience, kindness, goodness, faithfulness, gentleness, and self-control."[2]

The other important thing to remember is that we all have a purpose. God is perfect; He never has made and never will make a mistake. Psalm 139:16 tells us that He had a reason for our existence even before our birth: "Your eyes saw my unformed substance; in your book were written, every one of them, the days that were formed for me, when as yet there was none of them."

He has called us to salvation so that each of us may participate with Him in the work He is doing on earth: "In Him we have redemption through his blood, the forgiveness of our trespasses, according to the riches of His grace, which He lavished upon us, in all wisdom and insight making known to us the mystery of his will, according to His purpose, which He set forth in Christ as a plan for the fullness of time, to unite all things in him, things in heaven and things on earth" (Ephesians 1:7-10).

What an honor it is that the Lord of the universe has willed that we, His creation, might contribute to His grand design! No other person can fulfill the role that God has placed us in; He has guided our steps and established our connections in unique ways so that each of us has precisely the right resources to serve God's kingdom wherever God has us. "We might imagine that God's vision for the world is like a great jigsaw puzzle. You and I are the pieces in His hand, and He places us in just the spots where our particular shapes, sizes, and patterns best fit with the other pieces. The full picture only takes shape as all of the pieces come together in their proper places. In this view, no single piece is insignificant."[3]

~

In December of 2006, I retired from Goodyear and moved to Salem, South Carolina. My work as a corporate executive was finished, but God was just getting started with His purpose for my life. Although I was no longer in Ohio, I continued to serve as chairman of the board of trustees for Malone University in Canton until May of 2010. I drove back and forth for board meetings three times a year for those last three years.

At the end of my stint as chairman, I was given the opportunity to present the baccalaureate address at the 2010 graduation exercises; I was also presented with two plaques by the university. One of the plaques listed my name along with my years of service. The other featured a collage of pictures of the five buildings that were erected during my tenure as chairman at Malone. For a small university with limited funding, adding five new buildings in a twelve-year period is quite an accomplishment. That in and of itself is a testimony to the Lord's provision and the wonders that can be accomplished when we use His resources wisely.

Following in my dad's footsteps, I have made it my life's mission to glorify God through my labor, wherever of whatever that labor may be. After moving to South Carolina, my wife Gerri and I were called to the fellowship of Utica Baptist Church, part of the Southern Baptist Convention. Since joining the Utica Baptist congregation, I have had the opportunity to serve as a Sunday school teacher for adults, as a deacon, and as the chairman of the pastor search committee.

God has also allowed me to minister in the community outside my church fellowship. I served on the Board of Trust at Anderson University in Anderson, South Carolina, from 2010 through 2015; while there, I became the chairman of the institutional advancement committee of the board in 2013. I currently lead Oconee

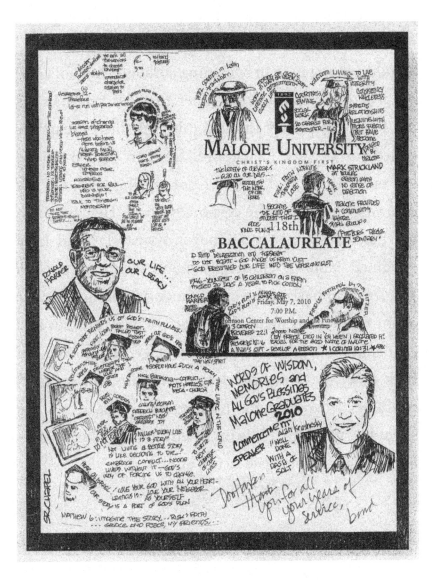

A graduating student captured the essence of the Malone
University 2010 commencement activities and messages with this
freehand drawing. I was honored to be the baccalaureate speaker.

Bible Study, an independent group of over a hundred people that meets weekly. I continue to mentor young men and families in an unofficial capacity. My passion is to guide young men in becoming authentic men of God.

It is important to remember that our purpose has not been completely fulfilled until our life on earth is ended. Just because I had retired from my regular job did not mean that I had retired from serving God. On the contrary, since I left the corporate world, He has grown my personal ministry far beyond what I could have imagined. James R. Gray, in his book *You Can Live Until You Die*, emphasizes the importance of making your life count right up to the end. He says, "Opportunities and challenges are available in every stage of life. We can walk away — or we can learn commitment, courage, readiness, and wisdom. As long as we have life, we should be growing."[4] It is my intention to do just that — pursuing God's purpose to the utmost.

~

1. *Have you ever struggled to be certain of God's will for your life? What did you do in that situation? How could you have acted differently?*

_____

_____

_____

_____

2. *Why do you think God opened the door for Don to become a professional baseball player? How does God want us to respond to opportunities?*

_____

_____

_____

_____

3. *In what ways was Don able to serve God through his career? Would he have been able to do these things if he had opted for the path to fame and fortune as a baseball player?*

_____

_____

_____

_____

4. *How does seeking God's will for your life grow your relationship with Him?*

_____

_____

_____

_____

5. *Philippians 1:6 says, "And I am sure of this, that he who began a good work in you will bring it to completion at the day of Jesus Christ." Do you believe that God is doing a good work in you? What work is He calling you to right now?*

_____

_____

_____

_____

CHAPTER TEN

LOOKING BACK, MOVING FORWARD

Every good story has a beginning, a middle, and an end. For most of us, the ending is the best part; it is when the bad guy gets his comeuppance, the good guy gets his reward, and everything comes together. For the ending to be truly satisfying, however, we have to see the hero's journey — the lessons he has learned, the struggles he has endured, and the progress he has made.

As God writes our stories, He knows exactly what experiences we need in order to grow towards a happy ending with Him; and when we look back at our lives and see how He has guided our journey, we can see how every twist and turn, every mountain and valley, has made the resolution so much sweeter. This account of the Harper family legacy ends where it began — with the purchase of the farm. It is necessary to see where my parents started in order to appreciate where God led them.

Both my parents were raised in stable, Christian

homes with both parents present. Their families share-cropped for their livelihood. Sharecropping was a system in which landowners who could not afford to pay laborers would rent out sections of their tenable land to families looking for work. The families would be responsible for cultivating the land, and the landowner would take a percentage of the crop as his due.

The system definitely favored the landowners. Because sharecroppers were cheap labor, many landowners made sure to give their workers only enough of the harvest to take care of their needs but not so much that the workers could save up and buy land of their own. The sharecropping system was implemented after the abolition of slavery in the United States, when landowners had suddenly lost their workforce and former slaves needed to establish themselves in a new way of living and working. Well up into the twentieth century, most African-American families living in the agricultural regions of the South worked as share-croppers rather than on their own land.

These were the days before welfare, when people did what they had to do to make a living. There weren't many career options available to a young African-American at that time. Most became schoolteachers, farm laborers, shop assistants, or domestics. Some enterprising individuals did create their own opportunities; for example, one of my aunts baked and sold pies for a living. As a whole, many of the available jobs required a higher education, and most young African-Americans did not have the resources to go to college.

Many African-American children quit school at a young age and began working to earn money to augment their families' finances. Both my parents did just that — Dad stopped going to school after third grade, and Mom stopped going after sixth grade. Neither of my parents ever pursued further education. Based on their upbringing and outlook at that point, it would not seem likely for either of them to ever advance beyond bringing forth a crop on someone else's property, but God had other plans for His two children.

In the first few years after my parents' marriage, Dad hired himself out for odd jobs on farms or in small businesses to make ends meet. My parents rented a house that probably had some land along with it on which to grow some vegetables to feed the family. Their first child, Josephine, was born in 1924, and the Harpers were a family of seven by the time the eighty acres became available. I think the fact that they had a growing family to provide for was a large part of what prompted my parents to aspire to more than the status quo.

As I mentioned before, my parents were married in 1923, and they did not purchase the farm until 1942. That meant they had to wait nineteen years for their dream to become reality. Their having to wait reminds me of the story of Abraham and Sarah; Abraham was seventy-five years old when God first promised that he would be the father of a great nation (Genesis 12:1), but Sarah did not give birth to their son, Isaac, until Abraham was almost a hundred (Genesis 21:5).

Did God forget His promise for twenty-five years? Not at all! Time and time again in Scriptures, God promised his children that something would happen, and it always did; however, the promises of God are not always fulfilled in the timing of man. Only God knows how all our tiny pieces fit into the big picture of the world's history and future, and therefore only He can determine the best time to make His promises come to pass. What He asks of us is faith that He will be true to His word.

This kind of faith goes far beyond common sense. As in the case of Abraham, circumstances often seem contradictory to God's purposes, at least for a time. In such situations, the world sees a believer's conviction as foolishness; however, God sees an obedient servant whose faith is to be honored, as is illustrated by Paul's description of Abraham in Romans 4:20-22: "No unbelief made him waver concerning the promise of God, but he grew strong in his faith as he gave glory to God, fully convinced that God was able to do what he had promised. That is why his faith was 'counted to him as righteousness.'"

One of the amazing things about the Christian life is that God does not just give us a series of goals and ask us to sustain ourselves between them; His work in our lives prior to the fulfillment of a promise is as purposeful as the promised outcome itself. Waiting on the Lord's next direction gives us time to learn and serve where we are. It also allows us to grow closer to the Lord, such that we can better see His glory in the work He is accomplishing through us.

In *Experiencing God*, Henry Blackaby describes the waiting process as an important time in the life of a Christian: "You may think of waiting as a passive, inactive time. Waiting on the Lord is anything but inactive. While you wait on Him, you will be praying with a passion to know Him, His purposes, and His ways.

You will be watching circumstances and asking God to interpret them by revealing to you His perspective. You will be sharing with other believers to find out what God is saying to them. [...] While you wait, continue doing the last thing God told you to do. In waiting, you are shifting the responsibility of the outcome to God — where it belongs."[1]

Sometimes we are blessed to see the result of God's perfect timing. For example, in the case of my parents, the farm opportunity came to them after they had several children old enough to help them care for it; if they had bought the farm right after they were married, the burden of keeping up eighty acres would have rested entirely on my dad, and he might not have been able to turn it into as successful an agricultural business as it was.

There are times when God's people do not get to see the fulfillment of God's promise within their lifetime. This might happen as a result of a lack of faith, as in the case of the children of Israel. God had promised that their nation would inhabit the land of Canaan, but the Israelites doubted God's ability to accomplish what he had promised when they heard a negative report from ten of their twelve spies. God kept his promise to the nation of Israel but judged those who had rebelled against His will, directing them to wander in the wilderness for forty years so that the only people who entered the Promised Land were those of the younger generation that had not grumbled against the Lord.

It is not always judgment that prevents believers from witnessing the fulfillment of God's promises; sometimes the big picture of God's purpose simply extends beyond the boundaries of our lifetime (or, at least, our awareness). For example, several generations of Jewish people came and went between the time that God spoke of the coming Messiah through His prophet Isaiah and the birth of Jesus Christ. Some members of those interim generations were, no doubt, sincere in their faith that a Messiah would come, but the timing was not yet right.

Thankfully, the God who sees past, present, and future simultaneously is directing not only *what* will happen in the course of earth's history but also *when* it will happen. Knowing that, regardless of when or how God's sovereign plan will be enacted, He will not fail to bring it to completion gives us peace for the moment and a hope for the future. Habakkuk 2:3 tells us, "For still the vision awaits its appointed time; it hastens to the end — it will not lie. If it seems slow, wait for it; it will surely come; it will not delay."

Knowing that God's timing is perfect, we must be attentive to His Spirit and ready to act when He directs us. My parents patiently waited on God to provide a place for them; and when He prompted them to move forward, they did not hesitate. They knew what effects a missed opportunity would have, not only on themselves, but also on their descendants.

~

Even after we grew up and moved away, the farm remained a special place for my siblings and me. Dad had saved up to build a nice house on the property after he and Mom purchased the farm, but it was designed in the fashion of an earlier time — there was no bathroom or running water inside the house. My sisters Lynn, Ruth, and Alyce provided funding to update the kitchen with a gas stove and to put in running water in the early 1960s. Even when they weren't living there to enjoy it, they did a great deal to keep up the house and make it comfortable for our family.

Mom passed away in 1991, and in 2010 my siblings

and I had to make the tough decision of what to do with the farm. The six of us who were still living at the time met in Birmingham to discuss our parents' vision for the farm and how best to ensure that their wishes would continue to be honored. Like Dad and Mom, we had to consider what would be best not only for ourselves, but also for our children and grandchildren. Since none of the family were in a position to resume full-time upkeep of the farm, we decided that the best thing to do would be to sell the property to someone who would cherish it and take care of it with the same passion that our parents had.

After all the arrangements had been made, my brother Robert sent out a letter to the family to explain the reasoning behind our decision:

Enjoying a moment with my son, Kevin, and other family members at the old home place.

To all of the Harper family (siblings, grand-children, great-grandchildren): The reason that you are sharing in a monumental experience is that God maybe tilted the scales in their favor such that they were able to purchase eighty acres of the best farmland in Perry County in 1942.

The South was very segregated in this era, and to find a banker willing to risk a mortgage on a man and woman who had no assets, no collateral, no full-time employment, no stocks or bonds, no portfolio, and no references was impossible to say the least.

Lloyd and Walter Mae were visionary enough

to realize that they needed to provide a safe haven in the segregated South to raise their children without exposing them to the 'Jim Crow' share-cropper mentality. The only way to do this was to try to purchase some

My mom, Walter Mae
Harper, in her later years.

fertile farmland in Perry County where they lived.

We were indeed blessed to be the children of two African-American pioneers who had the vision and internal fortitude to purchase land when the odds were definitely against them.

Lloyd had a true passion for the land and never wanted it to leave the ownership of the Harper family. In 1948, he prepared a complex will that provided for the land to transition from him to Walter Mae; and after her death, it was to transition to the eleven living siblings to share and share alike.

Our sibling base has been reduced to six, and we are not getting any younger, therefore we have decided to sell the land. We found a buyer who would carry on the dream that Lloyd and Walter Mae envisioned — that the land would be loved, preserved, and utilized for the good of mankind. The buyer will carry on the tradition of the land; twenty of the most fertile acres will continue to yield a grain crop, and most of the rest will be used for hunting and, in future, for building a home for another family member. I know Dad and Mom would just love that.

In memory of and dedication to Dad and Mom

and all my brothers and sisters, this has truly been
the experience and journey of a lifetime. I truly
thank Jefferson, Linzie, Ruth, Eleanor, and Don
for this opportunity; it will be with me forever. We
all believe that Dad and Mom would be proud to
know that what they started will be continued in
the future. What a dream, what a vision! We are
all so proud of the Harper name and its legacy.

~

That pride in the Harper name and legacy is
something that still endures and that I hope will continue
to endure in future generations. Lloyd and Walter Mae
Harper left behind a high standard for their children and
grandchildren to live up to; and now that the torch has
been passed, it is up to my siblings and me, and those
who come after us, to maintain a godly legacy.

I was very blessed to have such fine examples of
Christian living in my immediate family; I know that
not everyone is blessed in that way. Whether you are
carrying on a generations-long legacy of faith or are
breaking a pattern of brokenness and starting a new
story, know that you have a heavenly Father who loves

you and many generations of a family in Christ that have demonstrated what it is to live in the fullness of grace.

That is the true secret of leaving a godly legacy — being men and women of spiritual integrity in all phases of life. Philippians 3:13-16 says, "But one thing I do: forgetting what lies behind and straining forward to what lies ahead, I press on toward the goal for the prize of the upward call of God in Christ Jesus. Let those of us who are mature think this way, and if in anything you think otherwise, God will reveal that also to you. Only let us hold true to what we have attained."

Lloyd Harper, Sr.
January 1903 - October 1964

Walter Mae Harper
May 1906 - March 1991

Often what is emphasized in this passage is the need to forge ahead on a spiritual path, looking only to the future, but Paul points out that any progress must be made while keeping in mind what put us on the path in the first place — salvation through the sacrifice of Jesus. Live every moment overflowing with gratitude for what God has already done, joy for what He is doing, and hope for what He will do. That is a legacy that will endure.

~

1. How did Lloyd and Walter Mae Harper's humble beginnings make their farm purchase more meaningful?

_____

_____

_____

_____

2. What are some reasons that God would wait to fulfill a promise? What does He want us to do while we wait?

_____

_____

_____

_____

3. Is there anything that you are waiting on God to provide? How can you glorify Him in the meantime?

_____

_____

_____

_____

4. What are some ways that God has blessed you or stretched you in the past? How have those events shaped your life today?

_____

_____

_____

_____

5. What actions can you take today to build towards the future?

_____

_____

_____

_____

Notes

Chapter One
    1. Tozer, A.W. *The Knowledge of the Holy*. New York: HarperCollins Publishers, 1961. 103-6.
    2. Ibid. 72.

Chapter Three
    1. Schaeffer, Francis. *The Mark of the Christian*. London: Norfolk Press, 1970. 31.

Chapter Four
    1. Stearns, Richard. *The Hole in Our Gospel*. Nashville, Tennessee: Thomas Nelson. 2009. 3.

Chapter Five
    1. Piper, John. "How Do You Define Joy?" *Desiring God*. July 15, 2015. http://www.desiringgod.org/articles/how-do-you-define-joy.
    2. Piper, John. "What Is the Secret of Joy in Suffering?" *Desiring God*. August 6, 2015. http://www.desiringgod.org/articles/what-is-the-secret-of-joy-in-suffering.
    3. Lewis, C.S. *Reflections on the Psalms*. New York: Harcourt, Inc, 1958. 94-5.
    4. Ibid. 92.

Chapter Six
    1. Jeremiah, David. *Signs of Life*. Nashville, Tennessee: Thomas Nelson, Inc., 2007. 128.
    2. King, Martin Luther. *Strength to Love*. New York: Harper, 1963.

3. Jeremiah, David. *Signs of Life*. Nashville, Tennessee: Thomas Nelson, Inc., 2007. 130-1.

Chapter Seven

1. Colson, Charles and Nancy Pearson. *How Now Shall We Live?* Wheaton, Illinois: Tyndale House Publishers, Inc., 1999. 357.

2. Henry, Matthew and Thomas Scott. *Commentary on the Holy Bible*. Grand Rapids, Michigan: Baker Book House, 1960. 169.

3. Ibid.

4. Jeremiah, David. *Signs of Life*. Nashville, Tennessee: Thomas Nelson, Inc., 2007. 199.

Chapter Eight

1. Piper, John. *Don't Waste Your Life*. Wheaton, Illinois: Crossway Books, 2003. 32-33.

Chapter Nine

1. Blackaby, Henry T. and Claude V. King. *Experiencing God*. Nashville, Tennessee: Lifeway Press, 1990. 33.

2. Jeremiah, David. *Signs of Life*. Nashville, Tennessee: Thomas Nelson, Inc., 2007. 116.

3. Stearns, Richard. *The Hole in Our Gospel*. Nashville, Tennessee: Thomas Nelson, 2009. 150.

4. Gray, James R. *You Can Live Until You Die*. Greenville, South Carolina: Courier Publishing, 2015. 33-4.

Chapter Ten

1. Blackaby, Henry T. and Claude V. King. *Experiencing God*. Nashville, Tennessee: Lifeway Press, 1990. 142.

CPSIA information can be obtained
at www.ICGtesting.com
Printed in the USA
BVOW06s2337121216

470602BV00023BA/294/P

9 781940 645414